English

Assessment Practice

Book 1

Ages 10–11+ Years 5–6

Sarah Lindsay

OXFORD
UNIVERSITY PRESS

Great Clarendon Street, Oxford, OX2 6DP, United Kingdom

Oxford University Press is a department of the University of Oxford.
It furthers the University's objective of excellence in research, scholarship,
and education by publishing worldwide. Oxford is a registered trade mark
of Oxford University Press in the UK and in certain other countries

Text © Sarah Lindsay 2024
Illustrations © Oxford University Press 2024

The moral rights of the author have been asserted
Database right Oxford University Press (maker)

First published in 2024

All rights reserved. No part of this publication may be reproduced,
stored in a retrieval system, or transmitted, used for text and data mining,
or used for training artificial intelligence, in any form or by any means,
without the prior permission in writing of Oxford University Press,
or as expressly permitted by law, or under terms agreed with the appropriate
reprographics rights organization. Enquiries concerning reproduction
outside the scope of the above should be sent to the Rights Department,
Oxford University Press, at the address above

You must not circulate this book in any other binding or cover
and you must impose this same condition on any acquirer

British Library Cataloguing in Publication Data
Data available

ISBN: 978-1-382-05407-2

10 9 8 7 6 5 4 3 2 1

Printed in the UK

The manufacturing process conforms to the environmental
regulations of the country of origin

Acknowledgements

Content Development Adviser: Michellejoy Hughes
Page make-up: QBS
Cover illustrations: Lo Cole

Although we have made every effort to trace and contact
all copyright holders before publication this has not been
possible in all cases. If notified, the publisher will rectify
any errors or omissions at the earliest opportunity.

Contents

Welcome 4
A Note for Parents 5
How to Use This Book 6

Learning Papers

Comprehension 8
Grammar 1 12
Spelling 16
Vocabulary 1 20
Punctuation 25
Grammar 2 29
Sentences 32
Vocabulary 2 36
Curveball Questions 1:
Anagrams 39

Mixed Papers

Mixed Paper 1 40
Mixed Paper 2 44
Mixed Paper 3 51
Mixed Paper 4 58
Curveball Questions 2:
Formal language 62

Test Papers

Test Paper 1 63
Test Paper 2 70

Keywords 76
11+ Study Guide 78
Answers A1
Progress Chart A13

Welcome

Bond's English resources provide thorough and continuous practice for key English skills. They are ideal preparation for **Key Stage 1** and **Key Stage 2 SATs**, the **11+ and other selective school entrance exams**.

Bond offers a complete, flexible programme of preparation materials that you can adapt to your child's specific needs and to the requirements of the exam, or exams.

The 11+ exam is used by grammar schools and selective independent schools for entrance into Year 7. It assesses a child in verbal, non-verbal, English and mathematical reasoning, although individual schools may not test all four subjects, and they may combine some of the subjects together. The 11+ covers English and maths topics that a child will be familiar with from the National Curriculum, but supplements these with verbal reasoning and non-verbal reasoning questions.

Do remember to keep checking in with your school of choice so that you know which exam they are using. Schools change their exam boards from time to time. When sitting the actual test, there may be an additional time allowance for candidates needing additional support or an exam in a different format, so do also check with your prospective school if your child needs this. Every child has the right to access the 11+ exam and schools will do all that they can to support you.

Which Exam Board is this Book For?

Unless signalled on the front cover as being geared towards a specific exam board, all Bond 11+ materials are designed to hone the flexibility of approach essential to overcoming the challenges of any 11+ exam. The Bond system provides learning, information and consolidation so that children have an extended, rich education.

As different exam boards and schools may have different question types, the 11+ can be challenging to prepare for. This book can be used as preparation for all exam boards as it provides a wide selection of question types and an enriched education is the best preparation. Our aim is to familiarise children with the type of questions they will find in an exam and to give them the transferable skills that will allow a child to attempt any question in any exam. We help children to both master the techniques and develop the logic and rationale to tackle any unknown question types.

This all means that if you have been working towards an exam from a specific exam board and then the board used by your chosen school changes, all is not lost. This book is good preparation for whatever exam board is being used and the skills covered can be applied to any 11+ exam or independent school entrance exam. It is equally useful for pupils just looking for an extra challenge or wishing to prepare for secondary school.

A Note on Question Formats

The majority of 11+ exams now use multiple-choice answer format (where your child chooses their answer from a list of options), either entirely or for most of their questions. In Bond practice materials, your child will encounter both multiple-choice questions and some in 'standard format', which is where they have to write or type the answer into a box. We continue to use both because, whilst on the one hand it is good to practice in the format your child will face in the exam, standard format questions are proven to be more effective for learning and practice. When a child has to decide on an answer themselves without being given options, the simple act of writing out their answer makes their brain work a bit harder and helps those important skills to get stuck in their memory, ready to be used when they sit down for the real test itself.

How Else Can I Prepare for the 11+ Exam?

Bond has a wide range of books and resources to support learning. These include the *10 Minute Test* books and the *Puzzle* series. Bond Online provides a fun way for your child to consolidate their learning and we offer subscriptions which harness adaptive technology, perfect for building confidence.

KEY STUDY SKILLS

Working towards an entrance exam can be an exciting challenge. It is the chance to learn new things and to prepare for secondary school. Here are some tips to help your child:

- Create a study schedule so that they have a regular routine.
- Balance short bursts of practice with longer assessment papers.
- Create a quiet study space with pencils, an eraser, paper for working out, books and a notebook for writing down techniques. If they study in different places, keep everything in a box that they can take with you.
- Encourage your child to write down strategies to solve new topics.
- Limit distractions such as television, technology and games when they are studying.
- Remind your child that errors are useful. They are part of the journey to success.

A Note for Parents

Parents have a crucial role in helping children and motivating them. Here are some ways that you can really make a difference.

- Check your child is working at the right level. The goal is being able to score 85% on average. It's demotivating if they can't complete questions. It is also important that they work through the system so they are at the right level for the exam at the right time.

- Mark work promptly and go through errors. If papers have not been marked, a child has no idea how they are doing or whether they are repeating the same mistakes.

- Use the *Bond Handbooks* to help your child understand new techniques.

- Limit the range of homework you give your child. The best results are achieved by a system that gradually increases in difficulty. Completing lots of books and papers doesn't guarantee your child's success and often creates stress.

- If your child is struggling with something specific, add additional support in that area. Use *Bond 10 Minute Tests* for consolidation.

- Communication is key. Encourage your child to focus on the positive. No exam is going to ask for 100%, so pushing for that is unrealistic and stressful.

- If your child is constantly struggling, be realistic about whether a selective education is the right choice at this point in time. Many children move to a selective school for their GCSEs or A levels so not going to a selective school now doesn't mean they never will. It is about finding the best school for your child.

How to Use This Book

This book includes many step-by-step techniques for solving different question types. If further support is needed it can be used alongside one or more of the *Bond Handbooks*, which offer insights into the full range of questions that might occur in the exam.

- The first section of the book is made up of Learning Papers that focus on key skills with worked examples then lots of questions for consolidation.

- The second section of the book is made up of Mixed Papers so that children continue to consolidate and do not forget what they have learnt.

- The final section includes two full Test Papers, which can be broken down into shorter sections for more focussed practice, or can be used as full mock tests for that all important exam practice.

- There is an 11+ study guide at the back of the book with some useful hints and tips.

- The removable booklet attached to the back cover includes fully worked out answers to explain how an answer has been reached.

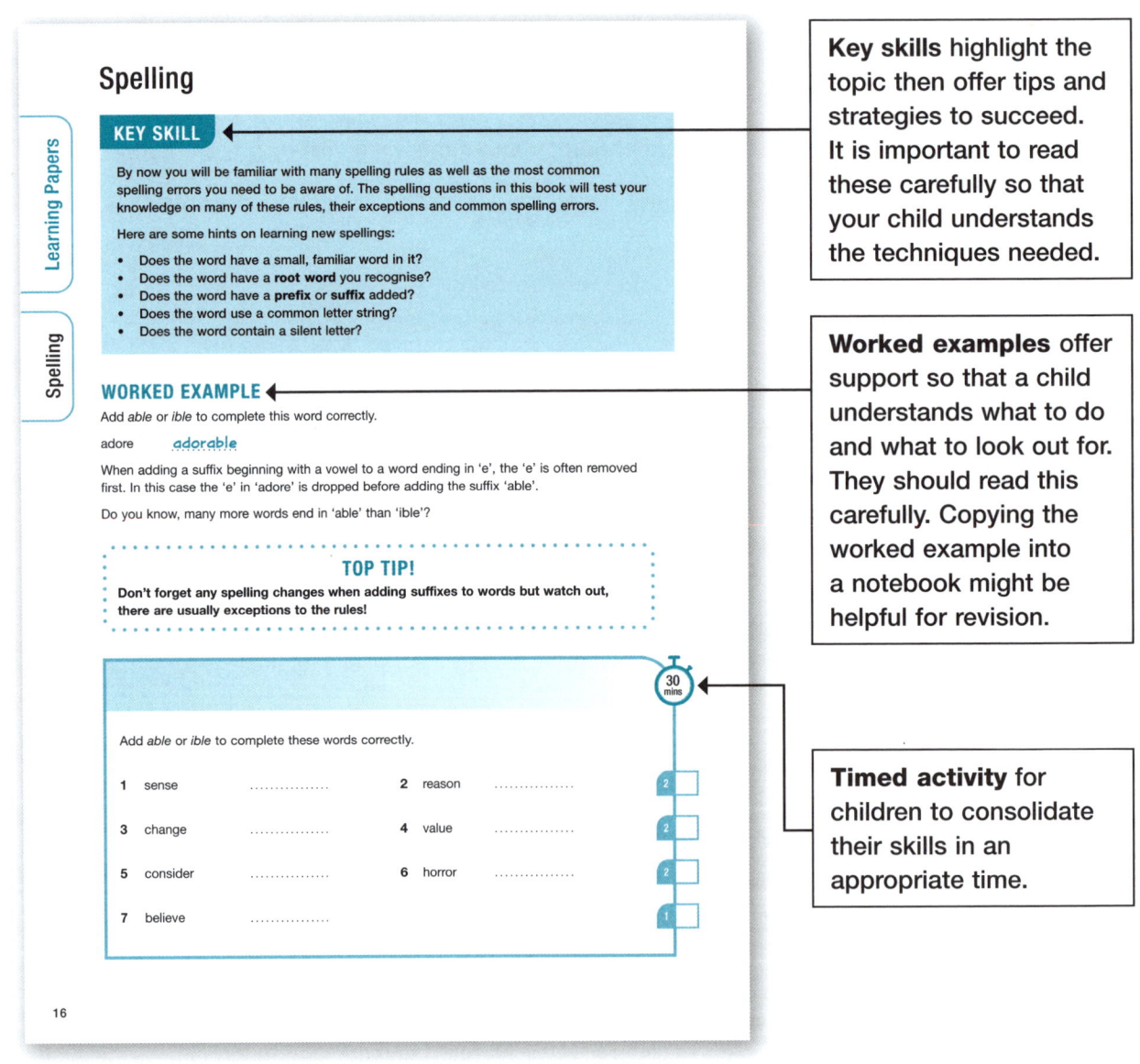

Key skills highlight the topic then offer tips and strategies to succeed. It is important to read these carefully so that your child understands the techniques needed.

Worked examples offer support so that a child understands what to do and what to look out for. They should read this carefully. Copying the worked example into a notebook might be helpful for revision.

Timed activity for children to consolidate their skills in an appropriate time.

KEY ENGLISH SKILLS

This Bond 11+ English Assessment Practice Papers book is useful for all 11+ exams. The learning papers cover the following key skills:

- **Comprehension** – a wide range of text styles, genres, and question types to test finding and retrieving, inference, and deduction skills.
- **Grammar** – including word classes, root words/prefixes/suffixes, spelling changes, tenses, and literary effects.
- **Spelling** – spotting incorrect spellings.
- **Punctuation** – spotting incorrect punctuation used in context.
- **Word choice** – choosing the correct word or group of words used in context

The Mixed Papers ensure the key skills are consolidated thoroughly, then the Test Papers give children the opportunity to get used to the exam process as a natural progression of each book. Don't forget that a rounded education is key. Your child should read as much as they can, play word games, do wordsearches and crosswords, listen to audiobooks, create a vocabulary notebook of words that they don't know and include antonyms and synonyms whenever they can – Bond has a set of Vocabulary Flashcards to help make this more fun. If your child is struggling to read a book, try a book of short stories so that they can read a whole story in one sitting. It is a great way to encounter lots of different authors. They could make a list of those they enjoy and then read their other books.
To build inference and deduction skills, encourage active participation. This is reading a paragraph or stopping a programme or movie at regular intervals and asking them to summarise what has happened. Ask what a character has done and why they might have done that. What do they think will happen next? Now read or watch some more and see if you were correct. As they get more information, their initial views might change and they may need to adapt their viewpoint.

Each book is part of the Bond system with books increasing gradually in difficulty. Once your child has completed this book, there is a clear progression in starting the next book age band if you child has an average score of 85% in this book. If they have achieved an average score of 70%–85%, then another book at this same age band will provide further support. If your child has achieved an average score of less than 70%, then moving down an age band will be most useful. Once your child has then developed the skills needed at this lower age band, they can then move up with confidence. It is often better to begin at a lower age band to build confidence as your child learns and develops their 11+ skills.

Learning Papers

Comprehension

KEY SKILL

Answering comprehension questions is like becoming a detective, looking at the evidence provided to find the clues that give you the answers.

Some questions require you to:

- look for straightforward information in a text (spotting);
- put answers in your own words (rephrasing);
- work out what has happened (deduction);
- read 'between the lines' to find meaning (inference).

All of these are important skills.

It is worth remembering that generally the more marks a question is worth, the more you are expected to write in your answer. Depending on the test, you may be asked to answer multiple choice and/or standard questions.

Multiple choice questions give you a choice of answers. You must select the one that answers the question the best.

Standard questions require you to search the text carefully to answer the questions.

Remember:

- Always read the text carefully.
- Always read the questions carefully.
- Read through your answers to check you have answered the questions correctly and clearly.

TOP TIP!

If you have time in the exam, read the extract twice. It is amazing what information you pick up when you read it through for a second time. It will also make answering the questions quicker as you will be more familiar with where to find the information.

Read this extract carefully.

Alice's Adventures in Wonderland

By this time she had found her way into a tidy little room with a table in the window, and on it (as she had hoped) a fan and two or three pairs of tiny white kid gloves: she took up the fan and a pair of the gloves, and was just going to leave the room, when her eye fell upon a little bottle that stood near the looking-glass. There was no label this time with the words DRINK ME, but nevertheless she uncorked it and put it to her lips. "I know something interesting is sure to happen," she said to herself, "whenever I eat or drink anything; so I'll just see what the bottle does. I do hope it'll make me grow large again, for really I'm quite tired of being such a tiny little thing!"

It did so indeed, and much sooner than she had expected: before she had drunk half the bottle, she found her head pressing against the ceiling, and had to stoop to save her neck from being broken. She hastily put down the bottle, saying to herself, "That's quite enough – I hope I shan't grow any more – As it is, I can't get out at the door – I do wish I hadn't drunk quite so much!"

Alas! it was too late to wish that! She went on growing, and growing, and very soon had to kneel down on the floor: in another minute there was not even room for this, and she tried the effect of lying down with one elbow against the door, and the other arm curled round her head. Still, she went on growing, and, as a last resource, she put one arm out of the window, and one foot up the chimney, and said to herself, "Now I can do no more, whatever happens. What will become of me?"

Luckily for Alice, the little magic bottle had now had its full effect, and she grew no larger: still it was very uncomfortable, and, as there seemed to be no sort of chance of her ever getting out the room again, no wonder she felt unhappy.

"It was much pleasanter at home," thought poor Alice, "when one wasn't always growing larger and smaller, and being ordered about by mice and rabbits. I almost wish I hadn't gone down the rabbit-hole – and yet – and yet – it's rather curious, you know, this sort of life! I do wonder what can have happened to me! When I used to read fairy-tales, I fancied that kind of thing never happened, and now here I am in the middle of one! There ought to be a book written about me, that there ought! And when I grow up, I'll write one – but I am grown up now," she added in a sorrowful tone; "at least there's no room to grow up any more here."

"But then," thought Alice, "shall I never get any older than I am now? That'll be a comfort, one way – never to be an old woman – but then – always to have lessons to learn! Oh, I shouldn't like that!"

"Oh, you foolish Alice!" she answered herself. "How can you learn lessons in here? Why, there's hardly any room for you, and no room for any lesson-books!"

And so she went on, taking first one side and then the other, and making quite a conversation of it altogether; but after a few minutes she heard a voice outside and stopped to listen.

by Lewis Carroll

WORKED EXAMPLES

Why was Alice pleased to find the bottle?

Alice was pleased to find the bottle as she hoped its contents might make her big again after she had previously been made small.

("I do hope it'll make me grow large again, for really I'm quite tired of being such a tiny little thing!" lines 7–8)

Write the letter that correctly answers the following question.

Who had been ordering Alice about? ......*C*......

A	B	C	D
her mother	fairies and mice	mice and rabbits	an old woman

In line 24 Alice refers to 'being ordered about by mice and rabbits'.

Answer these questions.

1. Write the letter that correctly answers the following question.

   Which of the following options is not a **synonym** for 'stoop' (line 10). ....

A	B	C	D
lean over	bend down	lower oneself	lay down

2. Which line in the passage suggests that Alice is not her normal size?

   ....

3. Is Alice worried about the rate she is growing? Find evidence in the passage to support your answer.

   ....

   ....

   ....

4. Give two reasons that explain why life was more pleasant at home for Alice.

   ....

   ....

5 Why do you think Alice might always have lessons to learn?

....

....

....

....

6 Alice debates with herself the pros and cons of never getting older (lines 31–33). Write two good things and two bad things that you can think of about never getting old.

....

....

....

....

....

....

....

....

7 What word class is the word 'outside' in line 37 [final sentence]?

....

8 Write two things Alice might have felt at the end of the passage as she stopped to listen.

....

....

....

Grammar 1

> ### KEY SKILL
>
> The following questions check your knowledge of the grammatical terms:
>
> **noun**   **pronoun**   **adjective**   **verb**   **adverb**   **preposition**   **conjunction**
>
> **Definitions** for these terms can be found in the Keywords section on page 76.
>
> Here is some additional information that can be useful to know.
>
> **Nouns** are naming words.
>
> There are different categories of nouns: **common** (table), **proper** (Thursday), **abstract** (enjoyment) and **collective** (flock). Make sure you recognise the differences between the types of noun.
>
> **Pronouns** can be used instead of nouns.
>
> A personal pronoun is a substitute for a person or people.
>
> For example, 'I', 'you', 'he', 'they', 'we', 'her'.
>
> A possessive pronoun shows ownership or possession.
>
> For example, 'his', 'mine', 'ours', 'theirs'.
>
> **Adjectives** describe a noun or pronoun.
>
> They might describe the colour, size or mood, for example 'green', 'huge', 'angry'.
>
> **Comparative** and **superlative** adjectives compare the difference between objects, for example 'larger', 'largest'.
>
> **Verbs** are doing and being words that tell us what is happening to the **subject** or noun in the sentence. The **tense** of a verb tells you when something is happening: present tense (happening now), past tense (happened in the past) and future tense (it is going to happen).
>
> Some tenses are formed using 'helper' verbs (auxiliary verbs).
>
> | to be | to have |
> |---|---|
> | I am running up the road. | I have run up the road. |
>
> **Adverbs** usually describe verbs. They describe 'how' (carefully), 'when' (early), 'where' (inside) and 'how often' (sometimes) something happens.
>
> **Prepositions** are used to link nouns and pronouns to other parts of a sentence highlighting 'time' (after), 'direction' (up) and 'position' (behind).
>
> **Conjunctions** are linking words that can be used to add information or make comparisons in sentences, **phrases** or words, for example 'for' or 'but'. Conjunctions can join two **clauses** in a sentence that help to improve the flow of your writing.

WORKED EXAMPLE

In this sentence write a **pronoun** for the **subject**.

Our football team won the cup.   subject pronoun   _they_

Our football team is the **subject** so the **pronoun** is 'they'.

In each sentence write a **pronoun** for each **subject**.

1. Ned hit the ball.   subject pronoun ....

2. The young girl cut her knee.   subject pronoun ....

3. The children in the school sang a song.   subject pronoun ....

4. The Patel family car hit a large pothole. subject pronoun ....

WORKED EXAMPLE

Add a **conjunction** to each of these sentences.

The children kept very quiet <u>while</u> their teacher was nearby.

'While' is the **conjunction** that is joining these two **clauses**. However other conjunctions could have been used, like 'as', 'because' and 'when'.

Add a different **conjunction** to each of these sentences.

5. Verity went home after dinner .... she wasn't feeling well.

6. The dogs waited for their walk .... the children put their coats on.

7. On Christmas Eve, Daniel couldn't fall asleep .... he was too excited.

8. Samina waited at the gate .... her mother arrived.

WORKED EXAMPLE

Write an interesting sentence, including an **adjective** and an **adverb**, using the **noun** and **verb** provided.

submarine   sank

The ageing submarine sank quickly as the sea poured into the damaged areas.

This sentence includes the **adjective** 'aging' describing the submarine and the **adverb** 'quickly' describing the **verb** sank.

Grammar 1

Write an interesting sentence, including an **adjective** and an **adverb** in each, using the **noun** and **verb** provided.

9 vase smashed

....

10 magazine opened

....

11 shark dived

....

WORKED EXAMPLE

Underline the **preposition** in the following sentence.

They threw the ball across the playground.

A **preposition** is a word that links a **noun**, **pronoun** or noun phrase to another word in the sentence. In this case the word 'across' relates to where the ball is being thrown.

Underline the **prepositions** in the following sentences.

12 Maria sat beside her friend Nareen.

13 They could not see beyond the hills.

14 Gareth threw the ball, and it went through the window.

15 Underneath the desk they found the rubber.

16 "Put the book on the table," Mum said.

17 The piano music was hidden under the pile of books.

WORKED EXAMPLE

Form a **noun** from the **verb** in bold to fill the gap.

invent   Her <u>invention</u> has proved very useful.

The **verb** 'invent' can be changed into the **noun** 'invention' by adding the **suffix** 'ion' to the **root word**.

Form **nouns** from the **verbs** in bold to fill each gap.

18 laugh   The .... of the crowd could be heard. [1]

19 solve   Tom found the .... to the problem. [1]

20 speak   Before he presented the prizes, the headteacher made an interesting
                    .... [1]

21 begin   The .... of the book was not very exciting. [1]

WORKED EXAMPLE

Underline the correct **verb** form, **singular** or **plural**, for each of these sentences.

Kate (<u>was</u>/were) very happy on holiday.

'Was' refers to one, 'were' refers to more than one; 'was' is therefore correct as it is referring to Kate and how she felt about the holiday.

> **TOP TIP!**
> It is often forgotten that 'was' and 'were', and 'is' and 'are' are verbs.

Underline the correct **verb** form for each of these sentences.

22 They (is/are) unsure whether to go to Pete's house. [1]

23 Meena and Tuhil (was/were) very excited about Diwali. [1]

24 The boys (was/were) keen to start the game. [1]

25 The coach (is/are) sure that they can win. [1]

Total 25

Spelling

> **KEY SKILL**
>
> By now you will be familiar with many spelling rules as well as the most common spelling errors you need to be aware of. The spelling questions in this book will test your knowledge on many of these rules, their exceptions and common spelling errors.
>
> Here are some hints on learning new spellings:
> - Does the word have a small, familiar word in it?
> - Does the word have a **root word** you recognise?
> - Does the word have a **prefix** or **suffix** added?
> - Does the word use a common letter string?
> - Does the word contain a silent letter?

WORKED EXAMPLE

Add *able* or *ible* to complete this word correctly.

adore   *adorable*

When adding a suffix beginning with a vowel to a word ending in 'e', the 'e' is often removed first. In this case the 'e' in 'adore' is dropped before adding the suffix 'able'.

Do you know, many more words end in 'able' than 'ible'?

> **TOP TIP!**
> **Don't forget any spelling changes when adding suffixes to words but watch out, there are usually exceptions to the rules!**

⏱ 30 mins

Add *able* or *ible* to complete these words correctly.

1 sense   ....   2 reason   ....   [2]

3 change   ....   4 value   ....   [2]

5 consider   ....   6 horror   ....   [2]

7 believe   ....   [1]

WORKED EXAMPLE

Write the **plural** form of this word.

butterfly   butterflies

'Butterfly' ends in 'y' so change the 'y' to an 'i' and add 'es' to make 'butterflies'.

> **TOP TIP!**
>
> **Rules to remember when making nouns plural:**
>
> **Add 's' to most nouns which end in a consonant or vowel.**
>
> **If a noun ends in 's', 'x', 'ch' or 'sh', add 'es'.**
>
> **If a noun ends in 'y', change the 'y' to an 'i' and add 'es'.**
>
> **If a noun ends in 'y' but the letter before the 'y' is a vowel, just add 's'.**
>
> **If a noun ends in 'f' or 'fe', change the 'f' or 'fe' to a 'v' and add 'es'.**

Write the **plural** form of these words.

8 computer ....   9 melody ....

10 knife   ....   11 yacht   ....

12 secretary ....   13 wolf   ....

14 garnish   ....   15 committee ....

WORKED EXAMPLE

Underline the correctly spelt word.

<u>preferring</u>   prefering

When adding **suffixes** to words ending in 'fer' there are rules to remember.

The 'r' is doubled if the 'fer' is still stressed when the ending is added.

However the 'r' is not doubled if the 'fer' is no longer stressed.

In this case, the 'fer' in 'prefer' is still stressed when 'ing' is added so the 'r' is doubled.

Circle the correctly spelt word.

16 refering   referring

17 reference   referrence

18 prefered   preferred

19 referal   referral

20 transference   transferrence

21 referree   referee

22 transferring   transfering

WORKED EXAMPLE

Add *ie* or *ei* to make a word.

c__ei__ling

Remember the rule: Write i before e except after c or if it sounds like ee.

TOP TIP!
There are exceptions to this rule. Watch out for them in these questions!

Add *ie* or *ei* to each of these to make a word.

23 perc __ __ ve   **24** n __ __ ghbour

25 l __ __ sure   **26** bel __ __ ve

27 rec __ __ ve   **28** dec __ __ ve

29 s __ __ ze   **30** ach __ __ ve

WORKED EXAMPLE

Rewrite this word, adding the missing silent letter so that each word is spelt correctly.

riggle   *wriggle*

Silent letters appear in many words but they are often before or after particular letters. In this case a silent 'w' is often followed with 'r', for example write, wring, wrote, wrestle.

Rewrite each word, adding the missing silent letter so that each word is spelt correctly.

31 hym ....

32 bom ....

33 nock ....

34 lim ....

35 wisker ....

36 autum ....

37 nelt ....

WORKED EXAMPLE

Underline the misspelt word and then rewrite it correctly.

<u>temprature</u>   thorough   twelfth   *temperature*

TOP TIP!
Don't forget to use a dictionary or spellchecker if you are unsure how to spell a word or are unsure of its meaning.

Underline the misspelt word and then rewrite it correctly.

38 signature   sufficiant   marvellous   ....

39 sacrifise   suggest   sincerely   ....

40 goverment   guarantee   privilege   ....

41 mischievous   necesary   nuisance   ....

42 recognise   desperate   vegtables   ....

43 curiosity   dictionery   controversy   ....

44 disasterous   hindrance   existence   ....

45 parliament   resturant   appreciate   ....

Total 45

Vocabulary 1

> ## KEY SKILL
>
> The more you understand about different types of vocabulary and its uses, the easier it is to make your writing more interesting. Here is a reminder of terms it is useful to be aware of:
>
> **Abbreviations** are a word or words which are shortened. Some abbreviations are commonly used, for example 'fridge' is an abbreviation of 'refrigerator'. Other types of abbreviations use the first letters of words; for example 'BBC' is an abbreviation of 'British Broadcasting Corporation'.
>
> **Alphabetical order** is important to understand when using a dictionary or thesaurus.
>
> **Antonyms** are words with opposite meanings, for example 'large' and 'small'.
>
> **Compound words** are words made from joining two or three separate **root words** to make a single word, usually with a different meaning to the individual words. For example, foot + ball = 'football'
>
> A **definition** explains the meaning of a word.
>
> **Homophones** are words that sound the same but are spelt differently and have different meanings. For example, 'deer' and 'dear'.
>
> **Root words** are the core words to which **prefixes** and **suffixes** are added to make other words. For example, 'comfort' is the root word in 'uncomfortable'.
>
> **Synonyms** are words that mean the same (or nearly the same). For example, 'huge', 'big' 'massive'.
>
> The following questions will check you have understood these.

WORKED EXAMPLE

Put these words in **alphabetical order**.

leather   learn   leave   least

learn   *least*   *leather*   *leave*

A technique for working out **alphabetical order** is to look at the first letters of each word. If the first letters are the same, we look at the second letters. If the second letters are the same, we look at the third letters. Once we get to a letter where there is a difference, we work out which comes first in the alphabet. In this case each word starts with the letters 'lea' so we are looking at the fourth letters to place them in the correct order.

Put these words in **alphabetical order**.

procure   procession   proclaim   proceed   process   processor

1 ....
2 ....
3 ....
4 ....
5 ....
6 ....

WORKED EXAMPLE

Write a **synonym** for the words in bold.

The twins were **exactly the same** in all ways.   identical

The phrase 'exactly the same' is a **synonym** for the word 'identical'.

Write a **synonym** for the words in bold.

7   The concert was **put off** until next week.   ....

8   She **made up her mind** to make a cake.   ....

9   The army **moved forward** to attack.   ....

10   They had a party **once a year**.   ....

WORKED EXAMPLE

Write the **root word** in this word.

trainer   *train*

The **suffix** 'er' has been added to the **root word** 'train' to form the word 'trainer'.

Write the **root words** in each of these.

11   bi-monthly   ....

12   pressure   ....

13   subdivide   ....

14   transatlantic   ....

15   disagreement   ....

16   endangered   ....

17   magical   ....

18   frightening   ....

WORKED EXAMPLE

Write an **antonym** for this word.

expand   *contract*

'Expand' means to increase in size; 'contract' means to decrease in size. They are **antonyms**. Other antonyms for the word 'expand' might be shrink, condense, decrease, diminish, reduce, dwindle or shrivel.

Write an **antonym** for each of these words.

19   inferior   20   mad   ....

21   question   22   divide   ....

23   reveal   24   elevate   ....

WORKED EXAMPLE

Match a word in each column to make a **compound word**. You can use each word only once.

~~green~~   look
day   knife
rain   light
water   ~~house~~
pen   knob
door   bow
out   tight

TOP TIP!
Put a line through the words as you use them.

greenhouse

The words 'green' and 'house' can be combined to make the word 'greenhouse'.

Match a word in each column above to make a **compound word**. You can use each word only once.

25 ....

26 ....

27 ....

28 ....

29 ....

30 ....

WORKED EXAMPLE

Write the **abbreviation** in full.

HGV   *heavy goods vehicle*

This **abbreviation** is formed from the first letters of the words being shortened.

Write the following **abbreviations** in full.

31 PTO ....

32 USA ....

33 MP ....

34 lol ....

WORKED EXAMPLE

Write a **definition** for this word.

obedient   *following orders or instructions, doing what you are told*

Remember, the **definition** of a word explains what the word means.

Write a **definition** for each word.

35 lubricate

.... [1]

36 minimum

.... [1]

37 summit

.... [1]

WORKED EXAMPLE

Write the **homophone** *there*, *their* or *they're* in the gap.

Where is *their* breakfast?

'Their' means 'belonging to them'. In this context the sentence refers to the breakfast that 'belongs to them' so 'their' is the correct **homophone** to use.

Write the **homophone** *there*, *their* or *they're* in each gap. Don't forget capital letters, if necessary.

38 They must get .... coats from over .... [1]

39 .... goes .... cat which .... giving away. [1]

40 .... always going to have queues if they don't open all .... tills. [1]

Total 40

Punctuation

> ### KEY SKILL
>
> Punctuation is used to make the meaning of your writing clear. Here are a few reminders:
>
> Commas (,) can be used to:
>
> - separate **clauses**
>
> The dog ran up to the gate, barking loudly, as the walkers approached.
>
> - avoid ambiguity
>
> "Shall we eat Laura?" becomes "Shall we eat, Laura?"
>
> - separate the speech in dialogue from the storyline
>
> "Let's go and get some lunch," suggested Amari, "because I'm getting hungry."
>
> - separate items in a list (but not before the last item)
>
> Odetta still had to collect some drinks, sandwiches, the dry towels and some money.
>
> When we write dialogue we use inverted commas (speech marks): " ".
>
> Remember:
>
> - Always make sure the spoken words are within the inverted commas.
> - The speech is finished with a comma, full stop, question mark or exclamation mark which comes before the second speech mark.
> - Each time the speaker changes, the dialogue starts on a new line.
>
> Apostrophes (') have two different jobs:
>
> - They replace missing letters in **contractions**.
> - They show belonging (possession).
>
> A semicolon (;) can be used between two **clauses** together.
>
> A colon (:) is often used before a list or quotation.

WORKED EXAMPLE

Write the two words this **contraction** replaces.

you're   you   are

The apostrophe is positioned where the letter 'a' in the word 'are' would be.

Punctuation — Learning Papers

⏱ 15 mins

Write the two words each **contraction** replaces.

1 I'm   ....   [1]

2 don't   ....   [1]

3 could've ....   [1]

4 it's   ....   [1]

5 they're   ....   [1]

WORKED EXAMPLE

Rewrite each of the following using only two words, one of which should have an apostrophe.

basket for a cat   *cat's basket*

There is one cat, so the apostrophe goes before the 's'.

If there was more than one cat sharing the basket the apostrophe would be placed after the 's'.

basket for the two cats   *cats' basket*

Rewrite each of the following, using only two words, one of which should have an apostrophe.

6 school for boys   ....   [1]

7 hostel for refugees   ....   [1]

8 garden for a dog   ....   [1]

9 canteen for the workers ....   [1]

10 barn for the cows   ....   [1]

26

WORKED EXAMPLE

Write a sentence using a semicolon.

Leah needed to go to Najib's house quickly; they had to get to football practice.

In this sentence the semicolon is used between two **independent clauses**.

> **TOP TIP!**
> The two clauses linked by the semicolon should be related to each other in some way.

Write a sentence using a semicolon.

11 .... [1]

WORKED EXAMPLE

Write a sentence using a colon.

Etta wanted to learn three instruments: the flute, violin and piano.

In this sentence the colon is used to introduce a list.

Write a sentence using a colon.

12 .... [1]

WORKED EXAMPLE

Punctuate this sentence correctly.

otti screamed look at that duck doing a headstand in the pond

Otti screamed, "Look at that duck doing a headstand in the pond!"

> **TOP TIP!**
> Make sure you add any missing capital letters. Every part of the sentence needs to be correct.

Punctuate these sentences correctly.

13 peter called im ready

.... 1

14 when will we get to nazar's house jake asked

.... 1

15 quick yelled sam we will miss our train

.... 1

WORKED EXAMPLE

Add the missing commas to this sentence.

After giving birth to three lambs**,** the sheep lay down**,** exhausted.

In this sentence the comma separates **clauses** and **phrases**.

Add the missing commas to these sentences.

16 Danielle the girl from number 12 sprinted speedily up the road. 1

17 Huw before leaving his house for the swimming pool collected his towel goggles and house key but forgot his swimming costume! 1

18 I jumped as high as I could flinging myself towards the lowest branch but collapsed on the ground from exhaustion. 1

Total 18

Grammar 2

KEY SKILL

Understanding the following increases your knowledge of how to write interesting and effective sentences.

Modal verbs are a type of verb that help other verbs by indicating the possibility of something happening. Some examples of modal verbs are 'can', 'will', 'must', 'shall', 'could' and 'should', and their negatives, 'can't', 'won't', 'mustn't', etc.

Sentences written in the **active voice** are used when the **subject** is performing the action. For example, 'The cat chases the leaf' – the subject 'cat' is doing the action of chasing the leaf. The active voice sounds more personal.

If this sentence was written in the **passive voice** it would sound more detached: 'The leaf is being chased by the cat.' The subject is now being acted upon by the verb.

An **adjectival phrase** adds more description to an **adjective**, using a group of words to describe a **noun**. It adds interest, context and colour to your writing. When trying to identify adjectival phrases look for a noun in the sentence. Sometimes there may be more than one noun. The **adjectival phrase** is the group of words that add description to a noun. For example, 'The dragon's large, red and menacing eyes terrified the explorer.'

A **fronted adverbial** is a word or phrase which adds extra information about the action that follows in a sentence and comes before a **verb**. Many fronted adverbials are single word **adverbs**, for example, 'Carefully', 'Immediately' or 'Later'. Some examples of phrases which are fronted adverbials are: 'In the distance', 'All of a sudden' and 'Without a sound'.

WORKED EXAMPLE

Write an **adjectival phrase** about this **noun**.

a car   *an old red, battered and rusty car*

This **adjectival phrase** gives more information about the car providing a clear picture of what the car looks like.

> **TOP TIP!**
> **One way of checking to see if you have correctly written an adjectival phrase is to ask yourself, 'Does the sentence still make sense if I remove the adjectival phrase?'**

Grammar 2

Write an **adjectival phrase** about each of these **nouns**.

1 an igloo   ....

2 a sandwich   ....

3 the sun   ....

4 a story   ....

WORKED EXAMPLE

State whether this sentence is written in the **active** or **passive voice**.

Tammy caught measles.   *active*

In this sentence the **subject** is doing something (catching measles); therefore the sentence is **active**.

State whether each of these sentences is written in the **active** or **passive voice**.

5 Daniel was frightened by the noise.   ....

6 The mouse was seized with fear on seeing the cat.   ....

7 Bola hit his head.   ....

8 The sweets fell out of the bag.   ....

9 The lorry damaged the gate.   ....

10 Jenny was bitten by the big dog.   ....

WORKED EXAMPLE

Write a sentence that begins with a **fronted adverbial**.

All day long, she played in the sand on the beach.

'All day long' is the **fronted adverbial** in this sentence as it gives more information about how long the girl played on the beach.

Write three sentences that begin with a **fronted adverbial**.

11 ....

12 ....

13 ....

WORKED EXAMPLE

Underline the **modal verb** in this sentence.

I <u>must</u> finish my homework tonight.

'Must' is the **modal verb** in this sentence as it suggests the possibility that the homework will be finished tonight.

Underline the **modal verb** in each of these sentences.

14 We might be able to go to the park after tea.

15 Shall I come to your house after school?

16 Jake wouldn't eat his breakfast before heading to school.

17 Aunty Zonda may be coming to stay this weekend.

18 Can I open the door, please?

Grammar 2

Total 18

Sentences

> ## KEY SKILL
>
> Here is some useful information on sentences:
>
> Sentences can be written as statements, questions or exclamations. They can be long or very short, but every sentence must include a **subject** and a **verb**.
>
> Sentences are built from **clauses** and/or **phrases**.
>
> Every sentence has a **main clause** with a subject and verb, but some may have more than one clause. These are called **multi-clause sentences**.
>
> Some multi-clause sentences are made of two main clauses, joined by a **coordinating conjunction** like 'and' or 'but'. These are **compound sentences**. In them, each of the main clauses (also known as **independent clauses**) can stand alone as a sentence. For example, 'Indira liked ice cream but Sanchia preferred chocolate.'
>
> Other multi-clause sentences are made of a main clause and a **subordinate clause**. These are known as **complex sentences**. A subordinate clause is a clause that gives more information about the main clause. It can't stand alone as a sentence and often starts with a **subordinating conjunction**. For example, 'Sanchia's chocolate melted because it was so hot.' Here, the subordinate clause is 'because it was so hot'.
>
> A **relative clause** is a type of subordinate clause. It describes a **noun** which has come before it and begins with a relative **pronoun**, for example 'that', 'which', 'where, 'who', 'whose'.
>
> **Indirect speech** sentences explain what has been said without using inverted commas (speech marks) to detail exactly what was said.
>
> Sentences with double negatives are important to avoid as their meaning becomes unclear.
>
> **Parenthesis** in sentences refers to additional information that isn't essential and therefore is highlighted using brackets, dashes or commas.

WORKED EXAMPLE

Rewrite this statement as a question, changing as few words as possible.

It is busy in town today.   *Is it busy in town today?*

Changing statements to questions often involves simply putting the words in a different order.

Rewrite these statements as questions, changing as few words as possible.

1 The weather is cold outside.

   ....

2 We should leave our football boots outside.

   ....

3 The dog enjoyed his walk on the moor.

   ....

4 We never use the old computer.

   ....

WORKED EXAMPLE

Write a sentence that indicates **parenthesis** using commas, brackets or dashes.

Come and enjoy the summer fair (which has now run for 20 years) and take part in all the fun activities.

In this case the additional information highlighted by the **parenthesis** is the amount of time the fair has run.

TOP TIP!
If you remove the information indicated by parenthesis, the sentence will still make sense.

Write two sentences that indicate **parenthesis** using commas, brackets or dashes.

5 ....

   ....

6 ....

   ....

WORKED EXAMPLE

Rewrite this sentence without double negatives.

There isn't going to be no queue at the cinema.

There isn't going to be a queue at the cinema.

This sentence has been rewritten with just one negative, now making clear its original meaning.

Rewrite these sentences without double negatives.

7 Damien didn't want no food.

.... [1]

8 There weren't no footballs in the shed.

.... [1]

9 There wasn't no water in the paddling pool.

.... [1]

10 Nina hadn't no problem with ice-skating.

.... [1]

WORKED EXAMPLE

Change the following sentences into **indirect speech**.

"Would you like to play football, Tim?" Jess asked.

Jess asked Tim if he would like to play football.

Remember, in **indirect speech** the actual words are not quoted, inverted commas are removed, and **verb tenses** may change.

> **TOP TIP!**
> Phrases such as '…said that…' or '…told them to…' are used to introduce indirect speech.

Change the following sentences into **indirect speech**.

11 Anil said, "I'll do my homework after I've watched television."

....

.... [1]

12 "I forgot to buy Anya a birthday present," Levi exclaimed.

....

....

13 "I'm afraid," Nan said, "it is time to go home."

....

....

WORKED EXAMPLE

Write a sentence that includes a **relative clause** using the **pronoun** 'which'.

Tariq opened a parcel, which had arrived before he left for school.

The **relative clause** in this sentence gives more information about the **noun** 'parcel'.

Write three sentences that include a **relative clause** using the following words.

14 that

....

....

15 which

....

....

16 who

....

....

Total **16**

Vocabulary 2

KEY SKILL

This section focuses on different literary techniques. Understanding these is particularly useful when improving the quality of your own writing, as well as answering questions relevant to literary techniques in comprehension extracts.

metaphor	an expression in which something is described as if it was something else (the words 'like' or 'as' shouldn't be used)
simile	an expression to describe what something is like
alliteration	the use of the same letter or sound at the beginning of words
personification	the use of human characteristics to non-human things
onomatopoeia	a word that represents a sound associated with its meaning
hyperbole	the use of exaggeration when it is known exaggeration is being used

WORKED EXAMPLE

Finish this **simile**, using your own words.

as light as *a feather*

Here, 'feather' is a good example of the **adjective** 'light', making this an effective **simile**.

TOP TIP!

Unlike a metaphor, a simile describes a noun using 'like' or 'as'. In these questions the similes use 'as'.

---

15 mins

Finish these **similes**, using your own words.

1 as pretty as .... [1]

2 as quick as .... [1]

3 as hot as .... [1]

4 as strong as .... [1]

5 as hard as .... [1]

6 as soft as .... [1]

WORKED EXAMPLE

Write two **onomatopoeic** words that can be associated with this word.

playground   *screech*   *argh*

An **onomatopoeic** word describes a sound. The words 'screech' and 'argh' imitate the sounds the children might make when playing in a playground.

Write two **onomatopoeic** words that can describe these words.

7 factory   ....

8 seaside   ....

9 zoo   ....

WORKED EXAMPLE

Complete this sentence as a **metaphor**.

The sea is a raging *lion*.

Any word that can be associated with the word 'raging' and makes sense works as a **metaphor**. Here the example 'lion' has been used but other words that can be used might be 'elephant' or 'beast'.

Complete each sentence as a **metaphor**.

10 The snow is a soft, white ....

11 The sun was a golden ....

12 The clouds are soft, fluffy ....

13 The wind is a howling ....

14 The stars were glittering .... in the sky.

Vocabulary 2

WORKED EXAMPLE

Read this sentence. State whether it is an example of **alliteration**, **personification** or **hyperbole**.

You could hear a pin drop.   *hyperbole*

This sentence is an example of **hyperbole** because it is exaggerating the sense of quiet suggesting you could hear a pin drop but in reality, you wouldn't be able to.

Read each sentence. State whether it is an example of **alliteration**, **personification**, or **hyperbole**.

15 The chocolate ice-cream called my name, so I had to buy one! 1

16 I was dying of laughter, watching the comedian. 1

17 Peter's prancing pony performed perfectly. 1

18 The alarm shouted at me to get up 1

19 I am freezing to death! 1

20 Lola likes licking liquorice lollies. 1

Total 20

Curveball Questions 1

Anagrams

KEY SKILL

An **anagram** is a word or **phrase** made by rearranging letters. It can be fun trying to solve what the intended word is. When trying to work out the word puzzle, always look for letters that sit comfortably together, for example, 'wh', 'er', 'est', etc. In the context of a sentence always read the sentence first as this might give a clue to the word you are looking for.

WORKED EXAMPLE

In each group of letters there is an item that you might find in the classroom. The letters have been jumbled.

SKED   *desk*

TOP TIP!

Despite how the letters are grouped together, remember they might make one or more than one word once solved.

Solve the riddles.

In each group of letters there is an item that you might find in the classroom. The letters have been muddled.

1 HECTARE ....   2 BOGLE ....

3 INDICATORY ....   4 WITHED BOAR ....

In the following sentences, a word has had a letter removed and the remaining letters have been muddled. Add the missing letter then rearrange the letters so that each sentence makes sense.

5 I ran out of the LITERATOR rain. ....

6 Leona felt DECEIT at the thought of going to the party. ....

7 Despite being scared, Moad was fascinated by PRIDES. ....

8 Clara checked her CANALED to see if she was free. ....

Total: 8

Mixed Papers

Mixed Paper 1

Punctuation

Add the missing commas to these sentences.

Example "No, I'm not going to the park after school," replied Tracy.

1 Daxa forgot the milk the bread and the tin of sweetcorn.

2 Today without realising it James was going to have the best day of his life.

3 Sarah stopped looked around and listened.

4 "Yes it's time to eat the party food" called Mum.

Rewrite these sentences, adding the missing punctuation and capital letters.

Example eram whispered are you awake
    Eram whispered, "Are you awake?"

5 the wind strong and gusty blew ninas hat off

   ....

6 the film is about to start yelled anton

   ....

7 the teacher said dont run in the corridor

   ....

40

Sentences

Write these sentences as **reported speech**.

Example "Get down from there," Kate called urgently to me.
Kate called urgently to me to get down.

8 "There's a knock at the door," mumbled Dad.

....

9 "Take Clawdie to the vet," Joe urged his parents.

....

10 "I'm going home now," Rosa declared.

....

Write two sentences that include a **relative clause** using the following words.

Example who *We are going to see our grandparents who live in the country.*

11 that ....

....

12 which ....

....

Vocabulary

Complete the following **similes**.

Example   as *dry* as sawdust

13 as .... as pie

14 as .... as a cricket

15 as .... as old boots

16 as .... as a cucumber

Write four sentences. In each sentence use the listed word or **phrase** correctly.

17 bird eating spiders

....

18 bird-eating spiders

....

19 recover

....

20 re-cover

....

Spelling

Complete these words, adding either *cial* or *tial*.

Example   essent*ial*

21 artifi...............

22 confiden...............

23 par...............

24 offi...............

TOP TIP!
Saying the words aloud will help to identify words according to their sound group.

Write four more words with the *ough* letter string. Each word must pronounce the *ough* differently.

Example   bought

25 ....   26 ....

27 ....   28 ....

Grammar

Add a different **conjunction** to each sentence.

Example   The sun was warm *although* it was December.

29 The children played in the pool .... the weather grew cold and windy.

30 I don't have to do it .... I don't want to.

31 He did not know .... his friend wanted to go swimming.

32 She was sent home .... she was not well.

Write whether each sentence is written in the **active** or **passive voice**.

Example   David climbed the tree.   *active*

33 The teacher called to the children.   ....

34 Ludka was hit by a snowball.   ....

35 The injured man was taken in the ambulance.   ....

36 Two cows pushed the gate open.   ....

37 The zoo keeper was bitten by the lion.   ....

Mixed Paper 2

Comprehension

Read the following comprehension text and answer the questions.

What is Climate?

Climate is different from weather, which can change quickly from day to day (or even hour to hour). Climate is the typical weather, winds, rainfall, and temperatures found in an area over tens or hundreds of years.

Different regions of the world possess different climates. Regions with polar climates
5   have long, cold winters and brief, cool summers whilst areas with a tropical climate are warm or hot all year round and receive a lot of rainfall. Scientists study and measure these climates and other factors, like the state of Earth's land and oceans, to get a picture of the planet's overall climate.

Earth is around 4.54 billion years old — imagine the candles on that birthday cake.
10 During its long lifetime, our planet's overall climate has changed many times. At times in Earth's history, it was so cold that ice covered North Africa where the Sahara Desert lies today.

Around 55 million years ago, it was so warm that instead of ice in the Arctic Circle, there were palm trees and crocodiles.

15 As you read this, Earth is in the middle of another change of climate, but what is causing so much worry is how fast it's changing. In the past, changes in climate have taken place naturally over thousands, sometimes millions, of years, but the latest change in global climate has taken less than 200 years to really get going. And, what's more, it's all our fault!

20 For thousands of years, people lived without affecting the planet's overall climate. **Then, from the 1750s, the Industrial Revolution changed things.**

Large numbers of factories, metal-making industries, and railways sprang up. All of these burned vast quantities of coal (and sometimes wood) to produce heat or to provide power via steam engines. Later industries and machines, like motor vehicles, burned
25 huge amounts of oil and natural gas as fuel. **All this burning sent gases up into the air.**

At the same time, the human population started growing fast and many forests were cleared to create more farmland to grow food to feed them. As well as food, these extra people required clothing and other goods, leading to more industry and factories. This all meant more burning and **emissions**—the word used to describe
30 substances that are released into the air.

All this activity has resulted in the entire planet's climate changing quickly. The average global temperature in 2020 was over 1.1°C warmer than 150 years before. That may not sound like much, but it's enough to **create BIG impacts**.

- Ice is melting.
35 - More droughts and floods are happening, devastating crops and communities.
- There are more extreme weather events like hurricanes.
- A warmer climate means more severe and longer-lasting wildfires.
- Sea levels have risen 21–24cm since 1870. They are predicted to rise far more in the years ahead.
40 - The changing climate is altering animals' habitats, making it difficult for many to survive.

It may all sound pretty grim, but there is still hope. People have solved many problems in the past—from combatting diseases to thinking up new ways to obtain energy. Ingenious inventions and schemes already exist to help reduce the damage
45 we're doing to the planet.

We just need to work together, really hard ... and quickly!

From *The Causes and Impact of Climate Change* by Clive Gifford

Write the letter with the correct answer.

1 Which of the following is not true?

    A Climate is different from weather.

    B Climate patterns change from day to day.

    C Climate is studied by scientists.

    D Different regions have different climates.

2 Why is it surprising that ice once covered North Africa?

....

....

3 How does the climate change happening now differ to previous climate changes on earth?

....

....

4 Between lines 26 and 30 (paragraph 8), copy a **phrase** that could be replaced with the word 'increasing'.

....

Mixed Paper 2

5 What are the two significant changes in the last 200 years that have affected climate change?

....

....

6 One of the big impacts of climate change is rising sea levels. What effect do you think this will have in some countries?

....

....

....

7 Read the final sentence again (line 46). Explain why we need to work together, work hard and work quickly.

....

....

....

....

Spelling

From the **verbs** listed write a **noun** ending in *ion*.

Example   lubricate   *lubrication*

8 produce   ....   **9** dictate   ....

10 create   ....   **11** resolve   ....

TOP TIP!
Saying the word aloud will help identify the stressed vowel.

2 mins

Underline the stressed vowel sound in each word.

Example vegetable

12 extra

13 regrettable

2

14 interest

15 temperature

2

Grammar

2 mins

In each space write the correct **preposition**.

Example That cake is similar to one that Dad makes.

16 Mr Kumar was very angry .... Tom when he broke the window. 1

17 David said that he did not like being accused .... being unkind. 1

18 The prize money is being divided .... Vish and his brother. 1

19 Mum said that she could rely .... me to do the shopping. 1

3 mins

In each space write a suitable **adverbial phrase**.

Example After the crash the rescuers worked quickly and quietly.

20 The whole class listened .... to their teacher. 1

21 A good worker does a job 1

22 To repeat malicious gossip is to talk 1

23 The children looked .... at the presents under the tree. 1

2 mins

Write which **tense** (past, present or future) the sentences are written in.

Example I am going to get my exam results today. future

24 The seagulls are enjoying the chips the family are feeding them. 1

25 When the rain arrived it soaked me to my skin. 1

Sentences

3 mins

Add a **clause** to each of these to make a longer sentence. Use a different **conjunction** each time.

Example Tom slipped, breaking his arm so we had to take him to hospital.

26 Tom slipped, breaking his arm ....

.... 1

27 Tom slipped, breaking his arm ....

.... 1

2 mins

Rewrite these sentences without double negatives.

Example Max didn't want no playtime.

Max didn't want playtime.

28 There isn't no shop open now.

.... 1

29 There aren't no penguins in the water.

.... 1

Vocabulary

Write an **antonym** for each of these words by adding a **prefix**.

Example   obedient   disobedient

30 correct   ....   31 aware   ....

32 probable ....   33 connect ....

Write the correct word or words next to each **abbreviation**.

Example   ml   millilitre

34 Prof.   ....

35 DOB   ....

36 Mr   ....

37 TBC   ....

Match the literary techniques with the correct sentences.

Example   The bedroom felt as cold as ice.   simile

alliteration   hyperbole   personification   onomatopoeia

38 The thunder groaned as the lightning danced.   ....

39 Husain hurried home to have some hummus.   ....

40 The traffic was a nightmare. 1

41 A buzz was heard from inside the tin. 1

Punctuation

Copy the words with the missing apostrophes and write them correctly.

Example "Ill get it," called Sam.   I'll

42 All was quiet when suddenly Kisha yelled, "Weve won a holiday!" 1

43 A swallows migration route finished in our shed. 1

44 Yasmin enjoyed a treat after shed finished her homework. 1

45 The pupils parents were coming to watch the show. 1

Write two sentences, each using a colon.

Example   I have picked up the following on my walk: a plastic bottle, a crisp packet and some bottle tops.

46 ....

....

47 ....

....

Total **50**

Mixed Paper 3

Comprehension

Read the following comprehension extract and answer the questions.

The Soup Movement

A nurse marched over to us. 'You should be resting, both of you. Come on, Rio, back to bed.'

Rio smiled sweetly at her. 'I'm just welcoming Ollie to the ward.'

'His name's Jordan,' the nurse replied.

5   'For now,' said Rio, ominously.

The nurse rolled her eyes. 'Back in that bed in five minutes, or you and I are going to fall out.'

'What's the matter with her?' I whispered to Rio once the nurse was out of earshot again.

10   'Kate's having a bad day,' she replied. 'I heard her at the nurse's station earlier. Split up with her boyfriend.'

I raised my eyebrows.

'Yeah, I don't miss a thing round here,' she went on. 'Got to do something to pass the time.'

15   Before I could reply, the little girl in the bed opposite mine had woken up and started crying. Her dad had just gone, probably to go to the toilet or get a drink, and she must have been scared. Straight away, Rio jumped out of the chair, went over and sat next to her. I couldn't properly hear what she was saying, but she picked up a couple of superhero action figures from the table and started putting on a little play, which
20   quickly made the little girl stop crying. She kept it up until her dad came back, then came back over to me and perched on the side of my bed.

'That was really nice of you,' I said.

Rio bobbed her head. 'It's all part of my new philosophy.'

'Philosophy?' I asked.

25   Rio leaned in closer to me, like she was letting me in on a deadly secret.

'There was a rabbi here yesterday,' she said. 'You know, like a Jewish priest kind of deal.'

I nodded, not sure where she was going with this story.

'We got to chatting and he told me about "mitzvahs",' she said. 'Do you know what a mitzvah is?'

30   'Isn't it a party where you get loads of money and people carry you around on a chair?' I said.

Rio shook her head. 'That's a Bar Mitzvah. A mitzvah is like a religious commandment, but it's also just doing something kind for someone.'

'OK,' I said, still confused.

35 'Well, I've been thinking about it,' she said. 'I was thinking that if everyone did mitzvahs for people whenever they got the chance, they'd pass them on and do more mitzvahs, and in the end, the whole world would be doing nice things for each other.'

To begin with, it sounded mad, but the more I thought about it, the more sense it made. I mean, when someone does a nice thing for you, it makes you feel better. Why
40 wouldn't you want to pass that on to someone else?

'Yeah, sounds good.'

'I know, right?' said Rio, a smile lighting up her face. 'So why don't we test my theory out by doing something nice for Moody Kate over there?'

Now I really saw where she was going. 'OK, like what?'

45 Rio jumped off the chair, then went back to her bed, reappearing a few seconds later with a couple of pieces of paper and a pencil case.

'We make her a card,' she said.

'What kind of card?' I replied. 'Like, "Sorry you split up with your boyfriend"?'

Rio shook her head. 'Too on the nose. How about, "Thanks for being great"?'

50 We quickly got to work making the card. I did the lettering, while Rio drew pictures of the two of us, holding flowers. She'd just finished drawing the inside illustration when Kate reappeared.

'What are you still doing here, Rio? I thought I told you to go back to bed.'

'Sorry, Kate,' said Rio, handing her the card. 'We were just making you something.'

55 Kate sceptically took the card, but when she looked at it, she started to smile, and her eyes went all twinkly.

'Thank you,' she whispered.

Rio glanced at me, a little smile on the corners of her lips.

'Look,' said Kate. 'Maybe you can stay up for a little longer. But only five minutes, OK?'

60 'That's very kind of you, Kate,' said Rio.

When she left, Rio looked at me with her hands out, like a magician revealing the grand finale of a magic trick. Then we watched as Kate stopped by the other beds in our bay, taking time to laugh and joke with the families.

'Wow,' I whispered.

65 'I know,' Rio whispered back. 'The magic of the mitzvah.'

I'm pretty sure she is the cleverest person I've ever met.

From *The Soup Movement* by **Ben Davis**

Write the letter with the correct answer.

1 Who is having a bad day?

    A Rio   **B** The little girl   **C** Kate   **D** Jordan

2 Which of these is not a **synonym** for the word 'sceptically' on line 55?

    A carefully   **B** dubiously   **C** suspiciously   **D** doubtfully

Answer these questions.

3 In line 5, we are told that Rio replies to the nurse 'ominously' in response to her questioning why she is calling Jordan 'Ollie'. What does this word suggest about Rio's intentions?

....

....

4 Rio goes and sits with the little girl in the bed opposite Jordan. Explain what her reasoning for this was. Use evidence from the text to support your answer.

....

....

5 In lines 35–37, Jordan is thinking about Rio's theory on kindness. Rio then says, 'Why wouldn't you want to pass that on to someone else?' (lines 39–40). What effect does asking this question have on Jordan?

....

....

....

6 In line 56, when Rio and Jordan give Kate the card, it states that 'her eyes went all twinkly.' What do you think this means?

....

....

....

7 After Rio and Jordan give Kate the card, Jordan says that Rio 'looked at me with her hands out, like a magician revealing the grand finale of a magic trick.' What type of literary technique has the author used here and what effect does it have?

....

....

Mixed Paper 3

....

.... [2]

8 In line 39, it says 'when someone does a nice thing for you, it makes you feel better.' Do you agree? Why?

....

....

....

.... [2]

Grammar

Match each word with its correct word class.

sharply   doubt   wrestle   they   heavy   gaggle   because

Example   adverb   *sharply*

9   **collective noun**   ....   [1]

10   **conjunction**   ....   [1]

11   **pronoun**   ....   [1]

12   **verb**   ....   [1]

13   **adjective**   ....   [1]

14   **abstract noun**   ....   [1]

TOP TIP!
Remember to start a new line when a different person starts to speak.

Punctuation

Rewrite the passage correctly.

15 Where are we going asked a shivering Ben To the haunted house replied Danielle I haven't got my boots on and we have to cross the stream exclaimed Ben Never mind Danielle laughed

"Where are we going?" asked a shivering Ben.

Finish this sentence. Include at least two semicolons in a list.

16 People enjoy playing sport for a number of reasons: ...

Sentences

Write two **multi-clause (complex) sentences**.

Example Aimee ran out the house because she was already late.

17 ....

....

18 ....

....

Vocabulary

Using a word from each column write four **compound words**.

~~home~~   weed
horse   roads
cross   cap
knee   shoe
sea   ~~work~~

Example   homework

19 ....   20 ....

21 ....   22 ....

Write the **root word** in each word.

Example   selfish   self

23 pressure   ....   24 heightened   ....

25 collapsible   ....   26 signatory   ....

Write two **definitions** for each of these words. One might be a meaning that has evolved over recent years.

27 cool

(1) ....

(2) ....

28 trainer

(1) ....

(2) ....

Spelling

Add a different **prefix** to each of these to make a new word.

Example   **dis**pleasure

29 .... ability   **30** .... sure   **31** .... plane

32 .... justice   **33** .... marine   **34** .... direct

Write the following **nouns** in their **plural** form.

Example   kangaroo   **kangaroos**

35 deer   ....   **36** knife   ....

37 mosquito   ....   **38** atlas   ....

39 ox   ....   **40** chief   ....

Mixed Paper 4

Grammar

Form **adjectives** from the words in bold.

Example sense — He gave a <u>sensible</u> reply.

1. **Greece** — The .... olives tasted good.
2. **study** — She is a .... girl.
3. **energy** — It was an .... dance.
4. **angel** — She had an .... voice.
5. **triangle** — It was a .... piece.

Write two sentences that begin with a **fronted adverbial**.

Example All day long, she played at the beach.

6 ....

7 ....

Vocabulary

Write these words in **alphabetical order**.

extinction   extra   extreme   extend   extract

<u>extend</u>   8 ....   9 ....

          10 ....   11 ....

Write a **metaphor** related to each of these **nouns**.

Example   sun   a golden ball

12 snow   ....

13 rain   ....

14 grass   ....

15 autumn trees   ....

Write a **definition** for each of these words used in **formal** writing.

Example   viewpoint   a point of view

16 argument   ....

17 conclusion   ....

18 opinion   ....

Complete each gap with the **homophone** *to, too* or *two*.

19 For Stan's dare he is going .... climb on the wall, take ....
steps and then run .... the growling dog and pat him on the nose!

20 It is .... hot .... play in the sun today.

21 The .... hens scratched around in the dirt, hoping .... find some food.

Anagrams

Unscramble the letters to find the missing word in the sentence.

Example   EIGHTH   The sudden *height* of the waves terrified the swimmers.

22   DECONS   Kyle felt devastated after coming .... in the race.

23   SWORD   She squinted at the tiny .... inscribed inside the ring.

24   RESCUED   The fragile sculpture was .... in place.

Spelling

The words below are wrongly spelt. Rewrite them correctly.

25   sufficent   26   definte   ....

27   resturant   28   programe   ....

29   pursuade   30   embarass   ....

Sentences

Rewrite the statement as a question.

31   You are going to check your answers before handing in the test paper.

....

Write a sentence using **parenthesis** correctly.

32 ....
....

Punctuation

Write two sentences. One sentence must use commas in a list; the other must use a comma after an introductory **phrase** or **clause**.

33 ....
....

34 ....
....

Rewrite each of the following, using only two words, one of which should have an apostrophe.

Example   hutch for rabbit   *rabbit's hutch*

35 tractors for farmers   ....

36 toy for a toddler   ....

37 parents for children   ....

Total 40

Curveball Questions 2

Formal language

KEY SKILL

Formal language is used in different contexts (letters, persuasive writing etc.). It is useful to be able to recognise formal language as well as use it in the correct scenarios.

Formal writing is not chatty and friendly in style. It is direct and to the point.

It doesn't use shortened forms of words. For example, 'tv' instead of television and **contractions** like 'wouldn't' are rarely used.

WORKED EXAMPLE

Write a more formal word for each of these **phrases** or words.

ask for   *request*

1 find out   ....   2 finish   ....

3 go in   ....   4 tell   ....

5 put forward   ....   6 say sorry   ....

7 Now write the following phrases in a passage that argues the case for or against the wearing of school uniform. Possibly also use some of the words you have written above.

    in contrast   as a consequence   on the other hand   my opinion

....

....

....

....

....

10 mins

Total 10

Test Papers

Test Paper 1

Read the following comprehension text and answer the questions.

Nathalie Sergueiew alias Treasure

Nathalie Sergueiew, alias 'Treasure', was a spy during the Second World War.

Sergueiew was one of many agents who double-crossed the German secret service during the Second World War. Between 1943 and 1945 Sergueiew's contacts in the *Abwehr* (Nazi Germany's counter intelligence organisation who managed the country's
5 spies and sabotage operations) believed her to be a loyal German spy. In reality, she was sending them deliberately misleading messages composed by the British secret service.

Nathalie Sergueiew was born in Russia in 1912. After studying in Paris she travelled around Europe, improving her mastery of several languages including German, French and English. In the mid-1930s she worked as a journalist in Germany. By the time the
10 war had started and she agreed to work for the *Abwehr*, she had already decided that her real loyalties lay with the Allies and she would do all she could to help them from within the German intelligence system.

Sergueiew met her *Abwehr* boss, Emil Kliemann, in Berlin and began to learn espionage skills such as secret ink writing, ciphers, radio telegraphy and how
15 to identify different Allied uniforms and equipment. She hinted to her German employers that they should send her to England. At the same time she told the British authorities that she intended to double-cross. In 1943 she arrived in England and was immediately interrogated by MI5, who gave her the alias Treasure.

It was vital to MI5 to make the communications sent by double agents to Germany
20 as convincing as possible. At first Treasure sent messages to Kliemann in secret ink or encoded letters, but later she used a radio transmitter set. She passed to him false information concocted by MI5 as part of an elaborate and successful deception plan to keep D-Day (the first day of the Allied invasion into Europe) secret. Treasure led Kliemann to believe that there were very few troops in South West England and
25 that she had a boyfriend in the 14th Army (a non-existent unit invented by the Allies). This information fitted in with messages from other double agents and supported the Germans' false belief that the Allies would land at Calais rather than in Normandy.

Treasure was an effective double agent but she was also known to be 'exceptionally temperamental and troublesome'. In conversations with her MI5 handler, Mary Sherer,
30 Treasure revealed that she had let slip her double identity to an American soldier. She also threatened to stop working for MI5 unless they arranged for her beloved pet dog left in Spain to join her.

One month before D-Day, Treasure admitted she had agreed a secret signal with her *Abwehr* contact, Kliemann, so he would know if her transmissions were genuine. This
35 meant that if another agent took over her transmissions, her cover would be blown, possibly putting at risk the whole network of double agents. Treasure was told that her services were no longer required because her behaviour endangered the Allies. The next day Sherer met with an upset Sergueiew, who suddenly said she would give Sherer the secret code agreed with Kliemann.

40 Sergueiew returned to France, but this was not the end of MI5's troubles. In 1944 it was discovered that she intended to publish her memoirs, in which she referred to her MI5 handlers as 'gangsters' and refused to hide their identities. The book was eventually published in 1968.

From www.nationalarchives.gov.uk/spies

Circle the letter with the correct answer.

1 Which is the closest **definition** to 'sabotage' (line 5)?

    A war plans   **B** deliberate destruction

    C accidental damage   **D** a hidden danger

2 Who was Kliemann?

    A her boyfriend   **B** her best friend

    C her MI5 handler   **D** her German boss

3 Which of these was an 'espionage skill' Sergueiew learned from the Germans.

    A flying aircraft   **B** disguised writing

    C creating disguises   **D** map reading

Answer these questions.

4 List two things in Sergueiew's past that made her suitable to be a spy for the British.

    ....

    ....

5 Why was Sergueiew given an alias (an alternative name) by the British?

    ....

    ....

    ....

6 Why do you think the name Treasure was chosen for Sergueiew?

....

....

[1]

7 Explain the role of a double agent.

....

....

[1]

8 Using evidence from the passage explain why D-day was very important to the Allies and the role Treasure had in supporting it.

....

....

....

....

[2]

9 In your own words, give two pieces of evidence to support the claim that Treasure was 'exceptionally temperamental and troublesome'.

....

....

....

....

[2]

10 List and explain three qualities you think a spy would have needed during the Second World War.

....

....

....

....

[3]

Test Paper 1

65

Form a **noun** from each of the **verbs** in bold.

Example   detect   The <u>detective</u> solved the crime.

11 acquaint   The girl made my .... at the bus stop.   [1]

12 imagine   Laith used his .... to write an excellent story.   [1]

13 pollute   The .... of the river was scandalous.   [1]

14 compete   One .... was late for the start of the race.   [1]

15 restrain   Dad acted with .... though he was very angry.   [1]

16 employ   I work for Mr Tang, who is a very kind ....   [1]

Write the **singular** form of each word.

17 torpedoes   ....   [1]

18 calves   ....   [1]

19 valleys   ....   [1]

20 sheep   ....   [1]

21 mice   ....   [1]

22 batteries   ....   [1]

23 foxes   ....   [1]

24 olives   ....   [1]

Add an additional **clause** to each of these **main clauses** using the **conjunctions** given in bold.

25 after The dog jumped into the water ....

....

26 until Ruth slept peacefully in her bed ....

....

27 before A parcel arrived for Ahmed ....

....

Add the **verb** *is* or *are* in each gap to make the passage correct.

28 Dan .... the tallest boy in the school. Everyone .... quite envious of him.

They .... nowhere near as tall.

In the following sentences, two words have had a letter removed and the remaining letters have been muddled. Add the missing letter then rearrange the letters so that each sentence makes sense.

29 It PRUDE with rain and unfortunately, I'd forgotten my RUBELLA.

....

30 We ran to join the queue before the expensive KITSET were SOD out.

....

31 Kyle ROWED hard at his project and was WADDER a prestigious prize.

....

Add *ary, ery* or *ory* to complete each word.

32 brib..........   **33** diction..........   **34** nurs..........

35 mem..........   **36** libr..........   **37** vict..........

38 discov..........   **39** ordin..........   **40** sal..........

Rewrite this passage correctly.

41 I can hear something whispered Sandra so can I confirmed Rassell what could it be

....

....

....

....

Write the **contraction** for each of these.

42 they are ....

43 should have ....

44 I have ....

45 we will ....

46 there is ....

47 will not ....

48 you are ....

49 do not ....

Add an **adjectival phrase** to these **nouns**.

50 the moon ....

51 the North pole ....

52 the night sky ....

Write six **synonyms** for the word *said*.

53 .... **54** .... **55** ....

56 .... **57** .... **58** ....

Underline the sentences that use formal, official-type language.

59–62 A form needs to be obtained from the Post Office.

You will be notified shortly.

Thanks for your letter; it was great to hear from you.

Please respond promptly.

Please can I ride my bike to the shop?

Users are requested to refrain from running by the swimming pool.

Write two sentences that begin with a **fronted adverbial**.

63 ....

64 ....

Total 80

Test Paper 2

Read the following poem and answer the questions.

The World Below the Brine

The world below the brine,
Forests at the bottom of the sea, the branches
   and leaves,
Sea lettuce, vast lichens, strange flowers and seeds,
5   the thick tangle, openings and pink turf,
Different colours, pale grey and green, purple, white,
   and gold, the play of light through the water,
Dumb swimmers there among the rocks, coral,
   gluten, grass, rushes, and the ailment of swimmers,
10 Sluggish existences grazing there suspended, or
   slowly crawling close to the bottom,
The sperm whale at the surface blowing air and
   spray, or disporting with his flukes,
The leaden-eyed shark, the walrus, the turtle, the
15 hairy sea-leopard, and the sting-ray,
Passion there, wars, pursuits, tribes, sight in those
   ocean-depths, breathing that thick-breathing air,
   as so many do,
The change thence to the sight here, and to the subtle
20 air breathed by beings like us who walk this sphere,
The change onward from ours to that of beings who
   walk other spheres.

by Walt Whitman

Circle the letter with the correct answer.

1 What is this poem about?

   A the world beyond the brink   **B** the world below the sea

   C tropical forests   **D** outer space

2 What is 'brine'?

   A a bridge   **B** fresh water

   C a kind of fish   **D** salt water

3 Which animal is 'hairy'?

    A the walrus   **B** the shark

    C the sea-leopard   **D** the turtle

Answer these questions.

4 Which two words describe creatures which hang motionless or move slowly?

....

5 At which level in the sea does the sperm whale play? ....

6 Describe in your own words the eyes of the shark.

....

7 Why is the water described as 'thick-breathing air'?

....

An extract from 'Sea'

I am patient, repetitive, multi-voiced,
Yet few hear me
And fewer still trouble to understand

Why, for example, I caress
5 And hammer the land.
I do not brag of my depths

Or my currents, I do not
Boast of my moods or my colours
Or my breath in your thought.

10 In time I surrender my drowned,
My appetite speaks for itself,
I could swallow all you have found

And open for more,
My green tongues licking the shores
15 Of the world

Like starved beasts reaching for men
Who will not understand
When I rage and roar…

by Brendan Kennelly

Now answer these questions about the poem 'Sea'.

8 Who or what is narrating this poem?

....

9 What is meant by line 10, 'In time I surrender my drowned'?

....

....

10 Describe how the sea is feeling. Which line illustrates this?

....

.... [2]

11 What is the main difference between these two poems?

....

.... [1]

12 Which of these poems do you enjoy more? Give two reasons for your answer.

....

....

.... [2]

Write these questions as statements changing as few words as possible.

Example   Is the tree safe to climb on?   *The tree is safe to climb on.*

13 Can you see Ned hiding behind the bench?

.... [1]

14 Is the fish and chip shop open?

.... [1]

15 Is the homework due in on Monday?

.... [1]

16 Can we go out and play in the snow?

.... [1]

Complete each word, adding the missing letter.

17 depend__ncy **18** excell__nce **19** convey__nce

20 dec__ncy **21** blat__nt **22** obedi__nce

23 confer__nce **24** confid__nt

Write whether each of these sentences is written in the **active** or **passive voice**.

25 Kim swam the channel. ....

26 The sheep were rounded up by the shepherd. ....

27 Laila kicked the football. ....

28 The field was flooded with water. ....

29 Kurt was collected from school by his dad. ....

30 Rowan caught Lilka's cold. ....

Rewrite the passage into sentences and adding the missing capital letters and punctuation.

31 alice screamed as rudi jumped into the pool she hated water on her face though she loved playing on the inflatables that is why she had wanted a swimming birthday party can you stop jumping near me please asked alice as water dripped from her nose if I have to laughed rudi

Test Paper 2

Add the missing apostrophes.

32 Seva wasnt afraid.

33 Ellie copied Hamzas home work.

34 Were going to get to Uncle Matts house before it is dark.

35 We could hear the puppies wails.

36 Whats the problem?

37 Jacks mum wouldnt let him play on his bike.

Write a **definition** for each word.

38 abbreviate ....

39 obedient ....

40 resolve ....

Write an **antonym** for the following words by changing the **suffixes**.

41 hairless .... **42** starry ....

43 useful .... **44** cloudless ....

Write an **abbreviation** for each of these.

45 New Zealand ....

46 Royal Society for the Protection of Birds ....

47	Save our souls	....	1
48	United Arab Emirates	....	1
49	Republic of South Africa	....	1

Write two sentences that each include a **modal verb**.

50 1

51 1

Copy these words adding the missing silent letters, so that each word is spelt correctly.

52	anser	....	53	reck	....	2
54	crum	....	55	tonge	....	2
56	lam	....	57	casle	....	2
58	rubarb	....	59	wite	....	2

Underline the word which is the same word class as the word in bold.

60	**never**	grand	flaky	walk	yesterday	me	1
61	**across**	jump	before	river	bridge	wood	1
62	**yours**	hers	friend	near	and	boy	1
63	**because**	reason	safe	hard	and	list	1
64	**I**	author	person	he	am	boy	1
65	**crossly**	girl	smart	foe	patiently	friend	1
66	**kindness**	pour	hot	hope	large	the	1

Total 80

Keywords

Some special words are used in this book. You will find them in **bold** each time they appear in the Papers. These words are explained here.

abbreviation	a word or words which are shortened
abstract noun	a word referring to a concept or idea *love*
active voice	when the main person or thing does the action
adjectival phrase	a group of words describing a noun
adjective	a word that describes somebody or something
adverb	a word that gives extra meaning to a verb
adverbial phrase	a word or phrase that makes the meaning of a verb, adjective or another adverb more specific, e.g. The Cheshire cat vanished *quite slowly,* beginning with the end of its tail
alliteration	the use of the same letter or sound at the beginning of words that are close together
alphabetical order	words arranged in the order found in the alphabet
anagram	a word or phrase made by rearranging letters
antonym	a word with a meaning opposite to another word *hot – cold*
clause	a section of a sentence with a verb
collective noun	a word referring to a group *swarm*
common noun	word that is a general name for a person, place, animal, thing or event.
comparative	a word that is used to compare two things
complex sentence	a sentence containing a main clause and subordinate clause(s)
compound word	a word made up of two other words *football*
conjunction	a word used to link sentences, phrases or words *and, but*
contraction	two (or more) words shortened into one with an apostrophe placed where the letter or letters are missing *do not = don't*
coordinating conjunction	a word to join two or more clauses or phrases of equal importance
definition	a meaning of a word
formal	following rules; polite
fronted adverbial	an adverbial that has been moved before the verb, e.g. *The day after tomorrow,* I'm going on holiday.
homophone	a word that has the same sound as another but a different meaning and spelling *right – write*
hyperbole	the use of exaggeration when it is known exaggeration is being used *He never stops talking.*
independent clause	a clause that can stand by itself as a simple sentence
indirect speech	what has been said without using the exact words or inverted commas (speech marks)
main clause	a clause in a sentence which makes sense on its own

metaphor	an expression in which something is described in terms usually associated with another *the sky is a sapphire sea*
modal verb	verbs that change the meaning of other verbs *can, will*
multi-clause sentence	a sentence that contains two or more clauses
noun	a word used to identify people, places or things
onomatopoeia	a word that echoes a sound associated with its meaning *hiss*
parenthesis	a word or phrase that is separated off from the main sentence by brackets, commas or dashes usually because it contains additional information not essential to its understanding
passive voice	when the main person or thing has the action done to it *it was taken by him*
personification	the use of human characteristics to non-human things *The sun smiled down on the party.*
phrase	a group of words that act as a unit
plural	more than one *cats*
prefix	a group of letters added to the beginning of a word *un, dis*
preposition	a word that links a following noun, pronoun or noun phrase to another word in the sentence *the book on the table*
pronoun	a word used to replace a noun *he, she, they*
proper noun	the specific name of a particular person, place or thing *Ben, York, August*
relative clause	a special type of subordinate clause that makes the meaning of a noun more specific, e.g. The prize *that I won* was a book.
root word	a word to which prefixes or suffixes can be added to make another word un*well*
simile	an expression to describe what something is like *as cold as ice*
singular	one *cat*
subject	in an active sentence, the person or thing who does the action expressed by the verb *the lion roared*
subordinate clause	a clause that gives more information about, and is dependent on, the main clause
subordinating conjunction	a word or phrase that connects an independent clause to a dependent clause
suffix	a group of letters added to the end of a word *ly, ful*
superlative	describes the highest degree of a quality (adjective or adverb) *bravest, most beautiful*
synonym	a word with the same or very similar meaning to another word *quick – fast*
tense	used to show if a verb is in the past, present or future
verb	a word that can describe an action, state or feeling *run, keep, feel*

11+ Study Guide

Essentials

- Don't worry too much about the level that you start at. Beginning with an easier book can help your confidence.

- Make sure you have the right equipment – you will need your pencils, an eraser and a notebook.

- This book contains skills guidance and worked examples, but if you need more help with technique, the Bond Handbooks might also be useful to you.

Studying Effectively

1 Turn to the first topic and read the Key Skills box. You might want to read it a few times or with someone else to understand it properly or to underline key words.

2 Read the worked example a few times and make sure you understand it.

3 In your notebook, write down the topic heading and the worked example on a new page. This is for you to revise and remember. Once you have completed the final book, you will have a super-useful notebook that you can use in secondary school.

4 Now set a timer – a kitchen timer, a watch or phone with an alarm – for the timed section.

5 Work your way through the questions carefully. If you don't know the answer to something, draw a circle around the question number and take your best guess. This is important as you can find patterns if you make mistakes and it highlights where you need to consolidate.

6 Ask someone to mark the paper for you or mark it yourself and see where you made mistakes. Is there a common pattern? For every mistake, decide if it is not knowing the technique properly, not consolidating the technique enough or a loss of focus, and label this next to each question using T = technique, C = consolidation, F = focus.

7 Have another go at the questions you made errors in to understand what you did wrong. If it is a vocabulary problem, write down the word with its meaning / synonym / antonym at the back of your book so that you widen your vocabulary range.

Making Mistakes

Everyone makes mistakes and they are an important part of how we learn. The reason we practise before an exam is so that we can make those mistakes in a safe space rather than in the test itself and that way we can learn from them and make fewer mistakes when it really matters.

Remember that there is no such thing as a 'silly mistake'. You are not silly, and neither is your mistake. It is usually not understanding the technique, not consolidating the skill needed so that it is only partially remembered, or you have lost focus. Losing focus does not mean that you have done something bad; it just means that your attention was on something else. These tips can help:

Not Understanding the Technique:

- Go back to the learning section and reread the key skills box.
- Look at the worked example that you have in your notebook.
- Use the Bond Handbook for more support.

Not Consolidating Enough:

- It is amazing how much consolidation is needed by everyone so don't worry about doing lots of additional questions.
- Look at Bond online for some more questions to help you revise.
- Ask someone to test you on the technique.

Losing Focus:

- Make sure that you are not too tired, hungry, thirsty or distracted.
- Work out where you have made a mistake and break it down into sections. It might be that you focus on tricky division, but go too fast when it comes to addition. It might be that you read the comprehension extract, but you lost focus and misread it.
- Once you have identified the problem area, make sure that in new questions, you check yourself and focus carefully.

Common Problems

'I don't have time to study.'

Make sure that you have a timetable that is doable. If you have lots of activities that take up time, perhaps break your work up. The books all have timing sections so fit in smaller sections when you can. It's important to talk to your parent if you feel that you need more time for your 11+ work.

'I find it hard to complete my homework as I want to play instead.'

Motivation is difficult for most people. Don't completely stop all fun activities during the 11+ but get a balance. Key to this is a timetable so you know when, what and where to study. Make sure it is doable and build in something fun if you complete your homework for the day. Another tip is to write down your reasons for doing the 11+. It might be to keep your family happy, to get into a school that your friends are going to, or even that the school is convenient. Ask yourself how important each reason is. Can you commit to the reasons you have? If so, keep remembering the reason and what will happen if you don't commit. Perhaps talk to your family so that they know how you feel.

'My friend is using different books to me.'

The Bond 11+ system covers English/Verbal Reasoning and Maths/Non-verbal reasoning/spatial awareness. Bond has had many decades of success in 11+ material. Many tutors will only use Bond for their pupils, and they get an exceptionally high pass rate. It doesn't mean that Bond is the only 11+ provider, so don't worry that your friend is using different material. What is important is that you are fully prepared for your online exam, and you can have confidence in the Bond system.

'I'm scared of failing.'

It is natural to feel that. Remember that you cannot climb a mountain in one gigantic step. You need lots and lots of little steps to get to the top. The 11+ is like that. You can't sit down and learn everything straight away, but the little steps you take will lead you to the exam. Remember that every mistake can be identified and once you identify it, you may be able to understand it and solve the problem for next time. Mistakes are perfection in progress! If a selective school is the best learning environment for you, then you can work little and often through the books and then test papers leading up to the exam. If you find it too much and you are working at your full potential already, then maybe a school that is not selective will suit your learning better. There is no 'best school' and 'worst school' for everyone. It is the best school for an individual child. Do talk to someone about your feelings though as you need to feel supported.

'My friend has a tutor. Do I need one?'

Whether or not to have tutor depends on many different factors, including where your particular strengths and challenges lie, your own approach to learning, and whether the costs involved are feasible. The Bond system is rigorous and aims to support every child with a range of books and learning materials. The Bond Handbooks can do the job of a tutor and many tutors also use the Bond books and Handbooks with their pupils. Bond has been providing 11+ material since the 1960s, helping thousands of pupils to pass their 11+ exams without having a tutor.

'I don't want to do the 11+ exam.'

This is a conversation to have with your family, but the best advice might be to follow the 11+ books anyway. They will teach you skills, techniques and methods that will give you self-confidence regardless of the secondary school you attend. No knowledge is a waste, and you will be keeping your options open.

There is more information on the Bond website. Bond has a Parent's Guide to the 11+ and there is a range of supportive printed and online material. See online for further details. **www.bond11plus.co.uk**

Answers

Explanations in the main text of the book are referred to *by their page;* all other questions referred to can be found in the answer section.

Some questions will be answered in the children's own words. Answers to these questions are given in italics. Any answers that seem to be in line with these should be marked correct.

Learning Paper: Comprehension

1. **D lay down** A synonym is a word or words with a similar meaning. All the other options could be used in the sentence instead of 'stoop'.
2. *Lines 7–8 suggest Alice is not her normal size. "I do hope it'll make me grow large again, for really I'm quite tired of being such a tiny little thing!"*
3. *Yes, Alice is worried. In lines 11–13 she says to herself, "That's quite enough – I hope I shan't grow any more – As it is, I can't get out at the door – I do wish I hadn't drunk quite so much!" On line 19 she asks herself, "What will become of me?"*
4. *At home she didn't grow larger and smaller, and she wasn't ordered around by mice and rabbits (lines 23–24).*
5. *Alice feels that if she doesn't grow up, she will always have to do lessons. On lines 31–33 she says, "That'll be a comfort, one way – never to be an old woman – but then – always to have lessons to learn!"*
6. Any two reasons that are positive and any two reasons that are negative. Answers might include:
Positives – no health issues of being old, not dying of old age, having no responsibilities, being able to play, not having to pay bills, not having to run a home, not having to work.
Negatives – never being able to do what an adult does (travel, going to university, buying a house, buying a car etc.), having to learn lessons, always needing to be accompanied by an adult, not being able to be alone, not having choices, not having money.
7. **preposition** In this sentence the word 'outside' is a preposition; a word that relates other words to each other. In this case it tells the reader where the voice is being heard.
8. Any two reasons from the following:
Hopeful that someone is there who might help her, pleased that she will have someone to talk to, worried that she might be in trouble for drinking from the bottle or for being in the room.

Learning Paper: Grammar 1

1. **he** Ned is the subject.
2. **she** The young girl is the subject.
3. **they** The children are the subject.
4. **It** The Patel family car is the subject.
5–8. A conjunction is a joining word, such as 'and' or 'because', that joins two clauses together. Sometimes there is more than one conjunction that makes sense when joining two clauses.
5. Verity went home after dinner *because/as/since* she wasn't feeling well.
6. The dogs waited for their walk *while/as* the children put their coats on.
7. On Christmas Eve, Daniel couldn't fall asleep *because/as/since* he was too excited.
8. Samina waited at the gate *until* her mother arrived.
9–11. An adjective describes a noun and an adverb describes the verb or the adjective. Here are some possible answers:
9. *Mum's glass vase smashed noisily on the hall floor. The beautifully decorated vase suddenly slipped out of her fingers and smashed.*
10. *Jack opened his new magazine and eagerly began to read.*
Dad excitedly opened his travel magazine as he planned where to visit next.
11. *The hungry shark dived ferociously on its prey. The badly injured shark dived swiftly below the surface of the water.*
12–17. A preposition is a word that relates other words to each other. It gives information about where the noun is, i.e. its position.
12. **beside**
13. **beyond**
14. **through**
15. **underneath**
16. **on**
17. **under**
18–21. A verb is an action word. A noun is the name of a person, place or thing. Many verbs can be turned into nouns by adding a suffix; sometimes spelling changes are also needed.
18. **laughter**
19. **solution**
20. **speech**
21. **beginning**
22. They **are** unsure whether to go to Pete's house.
23. Meena and Tuhil **were** very excited about Diwali.
24. The boys **were** keen to start the game.
25. The coach **is** sure that they can win.

Learning Paper: Spelling

1–7. When adding a suffix beginning with a vowel to a word ending in 'e', the 'e' is often removed first.
1. **sensible**
2. **reasonable**
3. **changeable** This is an exception to the rule. If 'able' is added to a word ending in 'ce' or 'ge', the 'e' must be kept.
4. **valuable**
5. **considerable**
6. **horrible** The 'or' is dropped before adding 'ible'.
7. **believable**
8–14. The rules for making the nouns in these questions plural are detailed below, but remember there are always exceptions to these rules.
8. **computers** Rule: Add s to most nouns which end in a consonant.
9. **melodies** Rule: If a noun ends in 'y', change the 'y' to an 'i' and add 'es'.
10. **knives** Rule: If a noun ends in 'f' or 'fe', change the 'f' or 'fe' to a 'v' and add 'es'.

11 **yachts** Refer to Q8.
12 **secretaries** Refer to Q9.
13 **wolves** Refer to Q10.
14 **garnishes** Rule: If a noun ends in 's', 'x', 'ch' or 'sh', add 'es'.
15 **committees** Rule: Add 's' to most nouns which end in a vowel.
16–22 When adding suffixes to words ending in 'fer', the 'r' is doubled if the 'fer' is still stressed when the ending is added. However the 'r' is not doubled if the 'fer' is no longer stressed.
16 referring
17 reference
18 preferred
19 referral
20 transference
21 referee
22 transferring
23–30 In most cases, 'i' appears before 'e' except after 'c' or if it sounds like 'ee'.
23 perceive
24 **neighbour** (exception)
25 **leisure** (exception)
26 believe
27 receive
28 deceive
29 seize
30 achieve
31 hym**n**
32 bom**b**
33 **k**nock
34 lim**b**
35 w**h**isker
36 autum**n**
37 **k**nelt
38 sufficiant sufficient
39 sacrifise sacrifice
40 goverment government
41 necesary necessary
42 vegtables vegetables
43 dictionery dictionary
44 disasterous disastrous
45 resturant restaurant

Learning Paper: Vocabulary 1

1–6 To put these words in alphabetical order you need to look beyond the fourth letter in each word. Use a table to help you.

p	r	o	c	e	e	d		
p	r	o	c	e	s	s		
p	r	o	c	e	s	s	i	o	n
p	r	o	c	e	s	s	o	r
p	r	o	c	l	a	i	m	
p	r	o	c	u	r	e		

1 proceed
2 process
3 procession
4 processor
5 proclaim
6 procure

7–10 A synonym has a meaning that is the same, or very similar, as the phrase in the sentence. Here are some possible answers:
7 *postponed*
8 *decided*
9 *advanced*
10 *annually*
11 **month** The prefix 'bi' and the suffix 'ly' have been added to form the word 'bi-monthly'.
12 **press** The suffix 'ure' has been added to form the word 'pressure'.
13 **divide** The prefix 'sub' has been added to form the word 'subdivide'.
14 **Atlantic** The prefix 'trans' has been added to form the word 'transatlantic'.
15 **agree** The prefix 'dis' and the suffix 'ment' have been added to form the word 'disagreement'.
16 **danger** The prefix 'en' and the suffix 'ed' have been added to form the word 'endangered'.
17 **magic** The suffix 'al' has been added to form the word 'magical'.
18 **fright** The suffixes 'en' and 'ing' have been added to form the word 'frightening'.
19–24 An antonym has a meaning that is the opposite to the word given. Here are some possible answers.
19 *superior, better, grander, finer, greater, elite*
20 *sane, lucid, coherent, rational, balanced, stable*
21 *answer, reply, response*
22 *multiply, unite, unify, join, combine*
23 *hide, conceal, screen, disguise, cover*
24 *lower, drop, descend, decrease*
25–30 A compound word is a word formed from two other words.
daylight
rainbow
watertight
penknife
doorknob
outlook
31–34 Abbreviations are used to shorten words.
31 **Please Turn Over**
32 **United States of America**
33 **Member of Parliament or Military Police**
34 **laugh out loud**
35–37 The definition of a word explains what the word means. Here are some possible answers:
35 *to oil or grease something so that it moves easily*
36 *the smallest or lowest quantity*
37 *the highest point*
38–40 A quick way of remembering which word to use is that 'there' is connected to the words 'here' and 'where'. An apostrophe shows there are missing letters in a contraction so 'they're' is a shortened form of 'they are'. Finally 'their' means 'belonging to them'.
38 They must get **their** coats from over **there**.
39 **There** goes **their** cat which **they're** giving away.
40 **They're** always going to have queues if they don't open all **their** tills.

Learning Paper: Punctuation

1–5 Apostrophes replace missing letters in contractions.
1 **I am**
2 **do not**
3 **could have**

4 **it is** or **it has**
5 **they are**
6 **boys' school** There is more than one boy, so the apostrophe goes after the 's'.
7 **refugees' hostel** There is more than one refugee, so the apostrophe goes after the 's'.
8 **dog's garden** There is one dog, so the apostrophe goes before the 's'.
9 **workers' canteen** There is more than one worker, so the apostrophe goes after the 's'.
10 **cows' barn** There is more than one cow, so the apostrophe goes after the 's'.
11 A semicolon can be used to join two clauses together. For example:
Call me tomorrow; we can arrange a time to meet then.
12 A colon is often used before a list or quotation. For example:
I had all the things I needed to make biscuits: ingredients, utensils, baking sheets and an icing bag.
13 Peter called, "I'm ready." or Peter called, "I'm ready!"
14 "When will we get to Nazar's house?" Jake asked.
15 "Quick!" yelled Sam. "We will miss our train." or "Quick," yelled Sam, "we will miss our train."
16–18 Commas can be used to separate clauses or phrases, separate the speech in dialogue from the storyline and separate items in a list. In these questions it is to separate clauses and items in a list.
16 Danielle, the girl from number 12, sprinted speedily up the road.
17 Huw, before leaving his house for the swimming pool, collected his towel, goggles and house key, but forgot his swimming costume! (Comma after 'key' is optional.)
18 I jumped as high as I could, flinging myself towards the lowest branch, but collapsed on the ground from exhaustion.

Learning Paper: Grammar 2

1–4 An adjectival phrase adds description to a noun. Here are some possible answers:
1 *the icy cold igloo / the bright, white igloo / the frozen, shimmering igloo*
2 *the tasty cheese and tomato sandwich / the stale, uninspired sandwich / the usual cucumber and cheese sandwich*
3 *the hot, burning sun / the weak, milky-yellow sun / the blindingly bright sun*
4 *the incredibly funny story / a long, boring story / a short, snappy story*
5–10 In an active sentence, the subject is doing something ('the boy rode the horse'). In a passive sentence, the subject is having something done to it ('the horse was ridden by the boy'). The passive sentence often uses the word 'was' before the verb.
5 **passive**
6 **passive**
7 **active**
8 **active**
9 **active**
10 **passive**
11–13 A fronted adverbial sentence is a sentence that places the adverbial before the main verb. It is a word or phrase which adds extra information about the action that follows in a sentence. Here are some possible answers:
Before going out, pack your bag.
The week after next, we go on holiday.
Under the bed, he found a single shoe.
14–18 Modal verbs are a type of verb that helps other verbs by indicating the possibility of something happening.
14 We **might** be able to go to the park after tea.
15 **Shall** I come to your house after school?
16 Jake **wouldn't** eat his breakfast before heading to school.
17 Aunty Zonda **may** be coming to stay this weekend.
18 **Can** I open the door, please?

Learning Paper: Sentences

1 **Is the weather cold outside?**
2 **Should we leave our football boots outside?**
3 **Did the dog enjoy his walk on the moor?**
4 **Do we ever use the old computer?**
5–6 Parenthesis is the use of commas, brackets or dashes around additional information that is not essential to the rest of the sentence. For example:
The weather was beautiful, unusually for December, so we went out for a winter's walk.
Please phone the school office (the telephone number is on the website) or send an email letting us know your preferences.
When we get there – if we ever do – I shall show you the secret room.
7–10 Double negatives are when two negative words are used in the same sentence. Using two negatives turns the sentence into a positive one (which is confusing). There may be more than one answer for some of the questions.
7 **Damien didn't want any food.**
8 **There weren't any footballs in the shed. / There were no footballs in the shed.**
9 **There wasn't any water in the paddling pool. / There was no water in the paddling pool.**
10 **Nina hadn't got a problem with ice-skating. / Nina didn't have a problem with ice-skating. / Nina had no problem with ice-skating.**
11–13 In indirect speech (reported speech) the actual words are not quoted, inverted commas (speech marks) are removed, and verb tenses may change.
11 *Anil said that he would do his homework after he had watched television.* The words 'he would' and 'he had' may be written as 'he'd'.
12 *Levi exclaimed that he had forgotten to buy Anya a birthday present.* The words 'he had' may be written as 'he'd'.
13 *Nan said that she was afraid that it was time to go home.*
14–16 A relative clause is a type of subordinate clause (a clause that does not stand alone as a sentence but provides additional information to the main clause). It is used to modify the noun and often begins with the words 'who', 'that', or 'which'. Here are some possible answers:
This is the computer game that I bought last week.
She lives on the Wirral, which is in Merseyside.
That's the boy who lives near my aunt.

Learning Paper: Vocabulary 2

1–6 To make an effective simile you need to choose a word that is a good example of the adjective in the phrase provided. Here are some possible answers:
1 as pretty as a picture / garden / flower
2 as quick as a fox / cheetah / flash
3 as hot as fire/ a flame / chillies / pepper
4 as strong as an ox / a body builder / a digger
5 as hard as rock / stone / cement / nails
6 as soft as a duvet / cotton wool / a pillow

7–9 An onomatopoeic word is a word that describes a sound. The sound of the word imitates the sound being described, for example hiss, sizzle, pop, or bang. Here are some possible answers:
7 bang, whizz, pop, zoom, hum
8 splash, crash, splosh, caw, crunch
9 roar, growl, chatter, squawk, hiss

10–14 With a metaphor, we say something is something else. For example, the sun is a hot, gold coin. The words 'like' or 'as' shouldn't be used.
10 The snow is a soft, white pillow / blanket / marshmallow.
11 The sun was a golden ball / dish / coin.
12 The clouds are soft, fluffy cotton wool / tissues / feathers.
13 The wind is a howling wolf / dog.
14 The stars were glittering diamonds / sparkles / sequins in the sky.

15–20 To identify which literary technique is being used in these sentences you need to remember that alliteration uses the same letter or sound at the beginning of words; personification uses human characteristics for non-human things; and hyperbole uses exaggeration to make a point when it is known exaggeration is being used.
15 **personification**
16 **hyperbole**
17 **alliteration**
18 **personification**
19 **hyperbole**
20 **alliteration**

Curveball Questions 1

1 **teacher**
2 **globe**
3 **dictionary**
4 **white board**
5 **torrential** (missing letter 'n')
6 **excited** (missing letter 'x')
7 **spiders** (missing letter 's')
8 **calendar** (missing letter 'r')

Mixed Paper 1

1–7 Refer to pages 25–28 on Punctuation.
1–4 Commas can be used to separate clauses, separate the speech in dialogue from the storyline and separate items in a list.
1 Daxa forgot the milk**,** the bread and the tin of sweetcorn.
2 Today**,** without realising it**,** James was going to have the best day of his life.
3 Sarah stopped**,** looked around and listened.
4 "Yes**,** it's time to eat the party food**,**" called Mum.

5–7 Each correct sentence is worth two marks: one mark for correct punctuation and one mark for the correct use of capital letters.
5 The wind, strong and gusty, blew Nina's hat off.
6 "The film is about to start!" yelled Anton.
7 The teacher said, "Don't run in the corridor."

8–12 Refer to pages 32–35 on Sentences.
8–10 Indirect speech (reported speech) recounts what was said without quoting the actual words.
8 Dad mumbled that there was a knock at the door.
9 Joe urged his parents to take Clawdie to the vet.
10 Rosa declared that she was going home now.

11–12 A relative clause is a type of subordinate clause. It is used to modify the noun. Here are some possible answers:
Those are the dogs that live at number 34.
The coat, which fits me well, will keep me dry and warm.

13–20 Refer to pages 36–38 on Vocabulary. [V2]
13–16 A simile describes a noun using 'like' or 'as'. In this set of questions some are well-known similes but you can write your own version of a simile and it will still be correct as long as it makes sense.
13 as easy as pie / as tasty as pie
14 as chirpy as a cricket / as noisy as a cricket
15 as tough as old boots
16 as cool as a cucumber

17–20 These questions reinforce the difference between hyphenated words and non-hyphenated words. Here are some possible answers:
17 In the garden, the bird eating spiders looked happy with its catch.
18 Finn was amazed to read about the bird-eating spiders.
19 After the race, I had to lie down to recover.
20 I will re-cover both chairs once the decorating has been completed.

21–28 Refer to pages 16–19 on Spelling.
21–24 In most cases, 'tial' is used if it follows a consonant, and 'cial' is used if it follows a vowel. There are some exceptions.
21 **artificial**
22 **confidential**
23 **partial**
24 **official**

25–28 Each word with the 'ough' letter string must sound different. Here are some possible answers in addition to 'bought':
though, tough, drought, cough, through

29–37 Refer to pages 12–17 and 29–31 on Grammar. [G1 + G2]
29–32 A conjunction is a joining word that joins clauses together.
29 The children played in the pool *until/although/while* the weather grew cold and windy.
30 I don't have to do it *if/and/when* I don't want to.
31 He did not know *whether/if* his friend wanted to go swimming.
32 She was sent home *because/as* she was not well.

33–37 In an active sentence, the subject is doing something. In a passive sentence, the subject is having something done to it.
33 **active**
34 **passive**
35 **passive**
36 **active**
37 **passive**

Mixed Paper 2

1–7 Refer to pages 8–11 on Comprehension.
 1 **B Climate patterns change from day to day** Weather changes from day to day, climate is the pattern of change over many years.
 2 *It is surprising ice once covered North Africa as now it is where the Sahara Desert is.*
 3 *Climate change happening now is taking place so much quicker than previous climate changes that happened on Earth.*
 4 **growing fast**
 5 *The two significant changes for Earth were the industrial revolution and the increasing population.*
 6 *With sea levels rising, many coastal communities will be submerged, and wildlife will also be adversely affected.*
 7 *In order to slow the effects of climate change we need to work together to protect the planet, as individuals working alone couldn't make the scale of changes needed; work hard as many changes will require us to adapt our lifestyles; work quickly because the damage climate change is doing needs to be stopped fast in order to protect the planet.*
8–15 Refer to pages 16–19 on Spelling.
8–11 A verb is an action word. A noun is the name of a person, place or thing. Many verbs can be turned into nouns by adding a suffix such as 'ion', although sometimes spelling changes are needed.
 8 **production** Change the 'e' to a 't', then add the ending 'ion'.
 9 **dictation** Remove the 'e' and add the ending 'ion'.
 10 **creation** Refer to Q9.
 11 **resolution** Remove the 've' and add 'ute' to make the adjective 'resolute'. Then remove the 'e' and add the ending 'ion'.
12–15 The stressed vowel in a word is the vowel that is emphasised.
 12 <u>e</u>xtra
 13 regr<u>e</u>ttable
 14 <u>i</u>nterest
 15 t<u>e</u>mperature
16–25 Refer to pages 29–31 on Grammar. [G1]
16–19 A preposition is a word that relates other words to each other. It gives information about where the noun is, i.e. its position.
 16 **with**
 17 **of**
 18 **between**
 19 **on**
20–23 An adverbial phrase is the group of words that add description to a verb.
 20 *carefully and attentively*
 21 *thoroughly and with pride*
 22 *with a cruel tongue and spitefully*
 23 *longingly and hopefully*
24–25 The tense of a verb tells you when something is happening: present tense (happening now), past tense (happened in the past) and future tense (it is going to happen).
 24 **present**
 25 **past**
26–29 Refer to pages 32–35 on Sentences.
26–27 The clause that is added must have a main verb; otherwise it is a phrase. Here are some possible answers:
 Tom slipped, breaking his arm, but he was lucky not to harm himself too much.
 Tom slipped, breaking his arm because he had been running on the ice.
 Tom slipped, breaking his arm so he couldn't write anything for a month.
 Tom slipped, breaking his arm when he was playing ice-hockey.
 28 *There isn't a shop open now.*
 29 *There aren't any penguins in the water. / There are no penguins in the water. / No penguins are in the water.*
30–41 Refer to pages 20–24 and 36–38 on Vocabulary. [V1 + V2]
30–33 An antonym has a meaning that is the opposite of the word given. The prefixes used to create an antonym include 'in', 'im', 'un', 'dis' and 'mis'.
 30 **incorrect**
 31 **unaware**
 32 **improbable**
 33 **disconnect**
34–37 An abbreviation is a word (or words) which has been shortened.
 34 **professor**
 35 **date of birth**
 36 **Mister**
 37 **to be continued** or **to be confirmed**
 38 **personification** the use of human characteristics to non-human things, in this case 'the thunder groaned' / 'the lightning danced'.
 39 **alliteration** the use of the same letter or sound at the beginning of words, in this case <u>H</u>usain <u>h</u>urried <u>h</u>ome to <u>h</u>ave some <u>h</u>ummus.
 40 **hyperbole** the use of exaggeration when it is known exaggeration is being used, in this case 'a nightmare' to describe traffic.
 41 **onomatopoeia** a word that represents a sound associated with its meaning, in this case 'buzz'.
42–47 Refer to pages 25–28 on Punctuation.
 42 **we've**
 43 **swallow's**
 44 **she'd**
 45 **pupils' / pupil's**
46–47 A colon is sometimes used before a list or quotation.
 Before I go to school I have to do the following: brush my teeth, eat my breakfast and make my bed.
 Nina was furious: "How are he!"

Mixed Paper 3

1–8 Refer to pages 8–11 on Comprehension.
 1 **C** Kate is having a bad day because she split up with her boyfriend. The little girl had a bad moment when she woke and found her Dad wasn't there but the question specifically asked about 'a bad day'.
 2 **A** 'carefully' isn't a synonym (a word with a similar meaning) of 'sceptically'.
 3 *It suggests that Rio might have plans regarding the use of Jordan's name in the future. She is hiding something from Kate.*

4 Rio goes and sits with the little girl to be kind to her while her Dad is away. The text states Rio says, 'It's all part of my new philosophy.' (line 23)
5 By asking this question Rio isn't actually looking for an answer, she is stating clearly why wouldn't her theory work, which Jordan, having heard the question, acknowledges.
6 Kate having 'twinkly' eyes suggests that she was very touched and close to tears as when people start to cry (or fight back tears) their eyes appear to twinkle.
7 The author has used a simile, highlighting how Rio is stating how right she was where one kindness brings on another in a grand gesture.
8 The child's own answer stating whether they agree that doing something kind to someone can make you feel better and why they think this is so.
9–14 Refer to pages 12–15 on Grammar. [G1]
9 **gaggle** A collective noun is a word for a group of nouns.
10 **because** A conjunction is a word that joins clauses together.
11 **they** A pronoun is a word that replaces a noun in a sentence.
12 **wrestle** A verb is an action word.
13 **heavy** An adjective is a word that describes a noun.
14 **doubt** An abstract noun is a noun that describes a thought, feeling or idea.
15–16 Refer to pages 25–28 on Punctuation.
15 Each correctly punctuated sentence is worth one mark and each sentence started on a new line is worth one mark.
"To the haunted house," replied Danielle.
"I haven't got my boots on and we have to cross the stream!" exclaimed Ben.
"Never mind," Danielle laughed.
16 In a list, semicolons are used when there are already commas within the listed items, or when each item is several words long. Each semicolon used correctly is worth one mark. Here is a possible answer:
People enjoy playing sport for a number of reasons: to keep supple, through yoga or martial arts; to keep fit, through aerobic exercises such as running, cycling or rowing; for social benefits, through team games such as netball, football or cricket; and to develop new physical skills, through dancing, snooker, darts or skating.
17–18 Refer to pages 32–35 on Sentences. Each sentence should have two clauses, a main clause and a subordinate clause (another clause dependent upon it), joined with a conjunction. For example:
Darius fell in a puddle because he wasn't looking where he was going.
Mo fell off his scooter when he turned the corner too quickly.
19–28 Refer to pages 20–24 on Vocabulary. [V1]
19–22 A compound word is a word formed from two other words.
horseshoe
crossroads
kneecap
seaweed
23 **press**
24 **height**
25 **collapse**
26 **sign**
27 *cool* (1) a low temperature (2) fashionable or impressive
28 *trainer* (1) a type of shoe (2) a person who coaches sportspeople
29–40 Refer to pages 16–19 on Spelling.
29–34 A prefix is a group of letters added to the beginning of a word to modify its meaning. Some common prefixes include 're', 'de', 'dis', 'in', 'im', 'il' and 'un'. Here are some possible answers:
29 *inability, disability*
30 *unsure, insure, ensure, assure*
31 *monoplane, biplane, aeroplane*
32 *injustice*
33 *submarine, aquamarine, ultramarine*
34 *redirect, indirect, misdirect*
35 **deer** The word for the singular and plural is the same.
36 **knives** The spelling rule is to change the 'f' to a 'v' before adding 'es'.
37 **mosquitoes** The spelling rule is to add 'es'.
38 **atlases** Refer to Q37.
39 **oxen** This is an irregular plural. The noun is pluralised by adding an 'en'.
40 **chiefs** This is an exception to the 'swap the f to a v' spelling rule. In this case just add 's'.

Mixed Paper 4

1–7 Refer to pages 12–15 and 29–31 on Grammar. [G1 + G2]
1–5 An adjective is a word that describes a noun. We often use the suffixes 'able/ible', 'al', 'ful,' 'ic', 'ive', 'less' and 'ous' to make an adjective from a noun.
1 **Greek**
2 **studious**
3 **energetic**
4 **angelic**
5 **triangular**
6–7 A fronted adverbial sentence is a sentence that places the adverbial before the verb. Here are some possible answers:
Before going out, you need to pack your bag.
The week after next, we go on holiday.
As fast as you can, tidy your room.
8–11 A technique for working out alphabetical order is to look at the first letter. If the letter is the same, we look at the second letter. If the second letter is the same, we look at the next letter. Once we get to a letter where there is a difference, we work out which is first in the alphabet.
8–22 Refer to pages 20–24 and 36–38 on Vocabulary. [V1 + V2]
8 **extinction**
9 **extra**
10 **extract**
11 **extreme**
12–15 A metaphor says that something is something else. The words 'like' and 'as' are not used. Here are some examples:
12 *a white blanket, a mountain of feathers, a cover of salt, a cushion of sherbert*
13 *silver threads, bullets of steel, silver glitter, shards of glass*
14 *a green carpet, a felt mat, a patchwork duvet*
15 *coloured jewels, swaying feathers, dying embers, glowing flames*

16–18 Definitions similar to those given below are acceptable.
  16 *a disagreement, a reason put forward*
  17 *ending*
  18 *a belief*
19–21 Homophones are words that sound the same but have different meanings.
  19 For Stan's dare he is going **to** climb on the wall, take **two** steps and then run **to** the growling dog and pat him on the nose!
  20 It is **too** hot **to** play in the sun today.
  21 The **two** hens scratched around in the dirt, hoping **to** find some food.
22–24 Refer to pages 39–40 on Anagrams (Curveball Questions 1).
  22 **second**
  23 **words**
  24 **secured**
25–30 Refer to pages 16–19 on Spelling.
  25 **sufficient**
  26 **definite**
  27 **restaurant**
  28 **programme**
  29 **persuade**
  30 **embarrass**
31–35 Refer to pages 32–35 on Sentences.
  31 *Are you going to check your answers before handing in the test paper?*
  32 Parenthesis is the use of commas, brackets or dashes around additional information that is not essential to the rest of the sentence. For example:
  There is time to eat something – as you must be hungry – before we head out again.
  The dog, a regular visitor to the bins, was thought to be a stray.
  The road ahead is flooded (yet again!) but should be opened soon.
33–37 Refer to pages 25–28 on Punctuation.
33–34 Commas in a list, example: *He fed the cat, washed up, wiped and table and put the rubbish out.*
  Comma after an introductory phrase or clause, example: *Still reeling from the news, she opened the door.*
  35 **farmers' tractors** There is more than one farmer, so the apostrophe goes after the 's'.
  36 **toddler's toy** There is one toddler, so the apostrophe goes before the 's'.
  37 **children's parents** The word 'children' is plural already, so the apostrophe goes before the 's'.

Curveball Questions 2

1–6 All these answers are synonyms (words or phrases with similar meaning) of the words and phrases in the question.
  1 *discover*
  2 *complete*
  3 *enter*
  4 *notify / inform / request*
  5 *suggest*
  6 *apologise*
  7 There is one mark available for correctly using each phrase. The phrase **'in contrast'** must show an opposing point. The phrase **'as a consequence'** must show an effect from a cause. The phrase **'on the other hand'** must show a different effect from the same point. The phrase **'my opinion'** must be used to show a personal viewpoint. Here is a possible answer: ***In my opinion,*** *wearing school uniform is a good thing as every pupil looks the same, regardless of how much money a family has.* ***On the other hand,*** *it is true that buying a school uniform can be expensive for parents, as there are few places that sell suitable uniforms.* ***In contrast,*** *when children choose whatever they want to wear, a parent can pay as much or as little as they can afford. This does mean that some children may try to show off with new clothes all the time.* ***As a consequence,*** *it is easier to see who has more money and who does not, and school should not be about fashion and money.*

Test Paper 1

1–10 Refer to pages 8–11 on Comprehension.
  1 **B** Lines 4–5 state that Abwehr, a German counter intelligence organisation, managed sabotage operations, suggesting sabotage was planned and deliberate.
  2 **D** On line 13 it says that Sergueiew 'met her Abwehr boss, Emil Kliemann'.
  3 **B** On line 14 it states that the espionage skills Sergueiew learned included 'ciphers' which are codes – a disguised way of writing.
  4 Her language skills and her experience working in Germany as a journalist would have made her suitable as a spy. Sergueiew had 'mastery of several languages including German, French and English' and she had 'worked as a journalist in Germany' (lines 8–9).
  5 Sergueiew was given the alias Treasure so that her identity would not be compromised.
  6 She may have been given the name Treasure because the British felt she was a 'treasure' fulfilling the role of a double agent; or because the British may have felt that she was rare and special in her ability to work as a double agent.
  7 A double agent is a spy who works for one country while spying for another at the same time.
  8 D-Day was very important as it was the day the Allies planned to invade German-controlled land (line 23). Treasure was part of a trick to feed the Germans misinformation about where the invasion would take place (line 27), therefore making the invasion much easier for the Allies.
  9 Acceptable answers could include any two of the following points:
  She told an American soldier that she was a double agent (lines 29–30).
  She said she would stop helping MI5 if they didn't fetch her pet dog from Spain (lines 31–32).
  She set up a hidden code with Kliemann which showed her messages were really from her, but she didn't warn the Allies about this, which could have put her and other agents' lives at risk (lines 33–36).

10 Qualities such as bravery, adaptability, calmness, intelligence, discretion. Possible answers could include:
Bravery – a spy might have been discovered and either imprisoned or killed.
Discretion – a spy would have had to tell only trusted contacts what he or she knew.
Adaptability – a spy would have had to be able to adapt quickly to changes in circumstances.

11–16 Refer to pages 12–15 on Grammar. [G1] Many verbs can be turned into nouns by adding a suffix, though sometimes spelling changes are needed.
11 **acquaintance**
12 **imagination**
13 **pollution**
14 **competitor**
15 **restraint**
16 **employer**

17–24 Refer to pages 16–19 on Spelling.
17 **torpedo** To make the singular, remove 'es'.
18 **calf** To make the singular, remove 'es' and change the 'v' to 'f'.
19 **valley** To make the singular, remove 's'.
20 **sheep** Both the singular and the plural are the same.
21 **mouse** The singular and plural forms of this word are totally different.
22 **battery** To make the singular, remove 'es' and change the 'i' to 'y'.
23 **fox** Refer to Q17.
24 **olive** Refer to Q19.

25–28 Refer to pages 12–15 on Grammar. [G1]
25–27 The new clause that is added to the given clause must have a main verb; otherwise it becomes a phrase. Here are some possible answers:
25 *The dog jumped into the water after he had run the whole length of the beach.*
26 *Ruth slept peacefully in her bed until her alarm rang.*
27 *A parcel arrived for Ahmed before he went to school.*
28 Dan **is** the tallest boy in the school. Everyone **is** quite envious of him. They **are** nowhere near as tall.

29–31 Refer to pages 39–40 on Anagrams (Curveball Questions 1). Always remember to read the sentences carefully as they will give clues about the muddled words.
29 It **poured** with rain and unfortunately, I'd forgotten my **umbrella**.
30 We ran to join the queue before the expensive **tickets** were **sold** out.
31 Kyle **worked** hard at his project and was **awarded** a prestigious prize.

32–40 Refer to pages 16–19 on Spelling. It is worth remembering that of these endings, 'ary' is the most frequently used.
32 **bribery**
33 **dictionary**
34 **nursery**
35 **memory**
36 **library**
37 **victory**
38 **discovery**
39 **ordinary**
40 **salary**

41–49 Refer to pages 25–28 on Punctuation.
41 Each sentence that is written correctly should be awarded 2 marks; 1 mark for the correct use of all punctuation, and 1 mark for the correct use of capital letters. An additional mark should be awarded for starting a new line with a new speaker.
"I can hear something," whispered Sandra.
"So can I," confirmed Rassell. "What could it be?"

42–49 A contraction uses an apostrophe to highlight where letters are missing when words have been joined together.
42 **they're**
43 **should've**
44 **I've**
45 **we'll**
46 **there's**
47 **won't**
48 **you're**
49 **don't**

50–52 Refer to pages 29–31 on Grammar. [G2] An adjectival phrase describes the noun more specifically. Here are some possible answers:
50 *the glowing, crater-filled moon*
51 *the isolated, frozen North Pole*
52 *the starry, dark, expansive night sky*

53–58 Refer to pages 20–24 on Vocabulary. [V1] A synonym is a word that has a similar meaning. Here are some possible answers:
talked, muttered, whispered, shouted, reported, replied, cried, croaked, spoke, chatted, gossiped, mumbled, slurred, screeched, stated, responded, grumbled, conversed, nattered.

59–62 Refer to pages 62–63 on Formal Language (Curveball Questions 2).
<u>A form needs to be obtained from the Post Office.</u>
<u>You will be notified shortly.</u>
<u>Please respond promptly.</u>
<u>Users are requested to refrain from running by the swimming pool.</u>

63–64 Refer to pages 29–31 on Grammar. [G2] Remember, a fronted adverbial is a word or phrase that comes before a verb and gives more information about it, for example:
All of a sudden, the rain poured.
At 10 pm on Tuesday, Ali decided to phone Joe.
Without a sound, Holly crept downstairs.

Test Paper 2

1–12 Refer to pages 8–11 on Comprehension.
1 **B the world below the sea** Line 2 states that this poem is about 'the bottom of the sea'.
2 **D salt water** The title and line 1 state that the poem is about 'the brine'; the poem also includes many references to the sea, which is salty (unlike fresh water).
3 **C the sea-leopard** Line 15 refers to the 'hairy sea-leopard'.
4 The words *'sluggish'*, *'suspended'* and *'crawling'* are all appropriate. Lines 10 and 11 mention 'Sluggish existences grazing there suspended, or slowly crawling close to the bottom.'
5 *The sperm whale plays 'at the surface' (line 12).*
6 The shark's eyes could be described as *dark, heavy, solid* or *metallic* as these words all link with the description 'leaden-eyed' in line 14, and lead is a dark, heavy metal.

7 *The water is described as 'thick-breathing air' (line 17) because, to these underwater creatures, the water is like the air that humans breathe, but thicker.*
8 *The sea is the narrator of this poem. The poem, which is about the sea, is written in the first person using the words 'I' and 'me'.*
9 *Line 10 states that whatever has ended up in the sea, it will eventually be returned to the shore. Answers might refer to 'things' and 'items' but might also refer to people who are drowned. Both options are acceptable.*
10 *The sea feels misunderstood and lonely. This is shown in lines 2 and 3: 'Yet few hear me / And fewer still trouble to understand'.*
11 *The first poem is a description about life under the sea; the second is about the sea as a whole. The first poem describes the ocean and what lives in it; the second describes how the ocean feels.*
12 *The answer should state two reasons why one poem is preferred. For example:*
I like the first poem because it makes the ocean seem interesting and full of life. I also like it because it describes many different sea creatures and I can imagine them swimming about even though if I looked at the sea I wouldn't be able to see most of them.

13–16 Refer to pages 32–35 on Sentences.
13 **You can see Ned hiding behind the bench.**
14 **The fish and chip shop is open.**
15 **The homework is due in on Monday.**
16 **We can go out and play in the snow.**

17–24 Refer to pages 16–19 on Spelling. These can be tricky words to spell. Often there is confusion between using an 'a' or an 'e' in words with these endings.
17 depend**e**ncy
18 excell**e**nce
19 convey**a**nce
20 dec**e**ncy
21 blat**a**nt
22 obedi**e**nce
23 confer**e**nce
24 confid**e**nt

25–30 Refer to pages 29–31 on Grammar. [G2] In an active sentence, the subject is doing something. In a passive sentence, the subject is having something done to it. Passive sentences often use the words 'was' or 'were' before the verb.
25 **active**
26 **passive**
27 **active**
28 **passive**
29 **passive**
30 **active**

31–37 Refer to pages 25–28 on Punctuation.
31 Each sentence that is written correctly should be awarded 2 marks: 1 mark for the correct use of all punctuation, and 1 mark for the correct use of capital letters. An additional mark should be awarded for each new line started with a new speaker.

Alice screamed as Rudi jumped into the pool. She hated water on her face, though she loved playing on the inflatables. That is why she had wanted a swimming birthday party.
"Can you stop jumping near me, please?" asked Alice, as water dripped from her nose.
"If I have to," laughed Rudi. (or "If I have to!" laughed Rudi.)

32–37 Apostrophes are used to replace letters in contractions and to show possesion.
32 Seva wasn't afraid.
33 Ellie copied Hamza's homework.
34 We're going to get to Uncle Matt's house before it is dark.
35 We could hear the puppies' wails.
36 What's the problem?
37 Jack's mum wouldn't let him play on his bike.

38–40 The definition of a word explains what the word means. Here are some possible answers:
38–49 Refer to pages 20–24 on Vocabulary. [V1]
38 *to shorten*
39 *following orders or instructions, doing what you are told*
40 *to clear up something, or to decide to do something*

41–44 An antonym has a meaning that is the opposite to the word given. In this question, the antonym is formed by changing the suffix.
41 **hairy** The suffix 'less' is changed to 'y'.
42 **starless** The suffix 'y' is changed to 'less'.
43 **useless** The suffix 'ful' is changed to 'less'.
44 **cloudy** Refer to Q41.
45 **NZ**
46 **RSPB**
47 **SOS**
48 **UAE**
49 **RSA**

50–51 Refer to pages 29–31 on Grammar. [G2] A modal verb is a type of verb that can indicate the possibility of something happening, for example:
It <u>might</u> snow tomorrow.
My phone <u>must</u> be in my bedroom.

52–59 Refer to pages 16–19 on Spelling.
52 ans**w**er
53 **w**reck
54 crum**b**
55 tong**u**e
56 lam**b**
57 cas**t**le
58 r**h**ubarb
59 w**h**ite

60–66 Refer to pages 12–15 on Grammar. [G1]
60 **yesterday** The word 'never' is an adverb.
61 **before** The word 'across' is a preposition.
62 **hers** The word 'yours' is a possessive pronoun.
63 **and** The word 'because' is a conjunction.
64 **he** The word 'I' is a pronoun.
65 **patiently** The word 'crossly' is an adverb.
66 **hope** The word 'kindness' is an abstract noun.

Notes

Notes